THE CARNIVAL

Norma Iris Pagan Morales

ISBN 978-1-959895-76-3 (paperback)
ISBN 978-1-959895-75-6 (ebook)

Printed in the United States of America

Dedication

This novel is dedicated to my family members that are always there to give me full support in everything I do. Thank you, guys.

Introduction

People in Ponce, Puerto Rico, have been celebrating Carnival for over 250 years! Each year the Carnival lasts the whole month of February with parades, music, and special events.

The Carnival is a special celebration before the Christian season of Lent, the six weeks before Easter. During the Carnival, people make elaborated masks, dress up in costumes, dance, and play music.

The National Museum of American History is fortunate to have many Carnival-related artifacts generously donated by collector Teodoro Vidal.

Puerto Rico is an island, which means it is surrounded by water. Have you ever been on an island? Puerto Rico is located many miles off the coast of Florida.

Many years ago, a gentleman named Teodoro Vidal became a collector in Puerto Rico. He traveled all over Puerto Rico collecting artwork, furniture, toys, and much more. He collected many of the carnival masks and santos.

Overview

It all started at the Carnival in Ponce.

Alicia knew that there was drugs all over the place. Little did she know that by making an exclusive interview with the Narcos, she was risking her life and the rest of her crew.

David wasn't her cup of tea. She couldn't stand the guy. In the other hand, David was a sweetheart. He was always helping people in need.

He was usually called, GI JOE.

David had never cut it this close on a job before. His face and arms were covered in black paint. The black shirt and pants he wore were one of his standard uniforms, ones he'd been wearing for as long as he could remember.

As he crouched down behind the small air conditioning unit next to the recently renovated house, he swore he'd never cut it this close again.

He watched as the four men argued over the small body. Was the kid still alive? Even though it wasn't part of his guarantee for the job, he hoped so.

He had less than five minutes before the final call that would decide the fate of the boy. It was now or never.

Rushing from his position, he scaled the side wall in a blink of an eye, then quickly made it around the small house until he was standing at the back door. It took less than thirty seconds to open the locked door and even less time to make it to the end of the hallway.

Since he was in all black, he doubted the four kidnappers could see him in the darkened room. He was standing just two feet away from them, in plain sight, as the men continued to argue.

The leader, a short, balding man by the name of Gary, slammed his gun down on the table and told everyone to shut up. When the room was silent, Gary picked up a small cellphone from the table and dialed a number as he walked towards the back of the house.

As he spoke, David silently picked off each of the three remaining men.

He rushed behind the first and snapped his neck before the other two could respond. The second quietly went down with a quick punch to the throat. If Gary heard anything; it was only a quick intake of breath from the third man as David's knife slid silently into his throat.

Gary continued to talk on the phone as David picked up his gun from the table and pointed it at the back of the man's head.

"Move and you're dead, just like your buddies."

Gary tensed as he held the phone up to his ear.

"Commander here, the room is secure," David said to the room as Gary slowly dropped the phone to the floor in shock.

Just then, David heard a small noise behind him. As he turned to check what it was, Gary turned around with his fist and clocked him on the side of his ear.

David didn't even blink, but just looked at the shorter man and slowly wiped the blood from his ear.

"You shouldn't have done that." David used the butt of the gun to make a dent in the man's forehead.

As the man hit the floor in a heap of unconscious bad guy, David turned to see the eight-year-old boy lying on the table, staring at him like he was Superman.

"Are you a GI Joe?" the boy asked. David chuckled and thought about it.

"Sure, kid. Let's get you home to your dad." He walked forward and lifted the small boy from the table and carried him out into the night.

Contents

Chapter 1

Celebrating our Tradition

Juan Jose lives in Ponce, a beautiful town in Puerto Rico, where a month-long festival called Carnival is celebrated every year in February.

People dress up in bright costumes with papier-mâché masks resembling devilish animals, and hold "vejigas", colorfully painted balloon-like cow bladders.

The people who hold the "vejigas" are called "vejigantes", and they travel through the streets playing pranks on people.

Juan Jose has always been too young to be a carnival vejigante, but this year he is determined to join the bigger boys in the Carnival celebration.

For nine days he has secretly been making his first vejigante costume.

Let's find out what happens when Juan Jose goes to his first Carnival as a vejigante and the trouble he gets into after playing tricks on others.

Before I tell you the story about Juan Jose, let's look about the origin of the Carnaval….

There are no documents stating the official origin of the Carnival, but there are documents mentioning the celebration as early as 1858. El Carnaval de Ponce thus began in 1858 and was started as a mask dance by a Spaniard by the name of José de la Guardia.

The masquerade dance continued as a tradition through the years, but it was not until the 1950s that the municipal government added the parade to the Carnaval.

In the early 1960s, the Carnaval began to integrate floats that represented civic and cultural institutions, public and private residential communities, schools, colleges and universities, banking, industry, and commerce.

The Office of Cultural Development of the Municipality of Ponce explains that "it is believed that the influence of the Nice Carnival extended to Barcelona and that immigrants from Barcelona brought it to Ponce.

With the passing of time, Ponce have added their own touches with Afro-Antillean music that fills the celebrations with percussion, rhythm and happiness."

In June 1995, Carnaval de Ponce was taken to New York City where, during the Puerto Rican Day Parade, over 200 entertainers, folk artists, and musicians from Ponce, in addition to the Banda Municipal de Ponce and the Carnival's Queen and Child Queen, marched down New York's Fifth Avenue as part of that City's Puerto Rican Day Celebration.

During the week leading to the Parade, folk artists from the Carnaval de Ponce toured the city teaching children to make the traditional Ponce carnival's masks.

In 2012, a local news weekly called Carnaval de Ponce "Puerto Rico's National Carnival".

One of the traditions of the Carnaval is the appearance of the "vejigantes", which is a colorful costume traditionally representing the devil or evil. Vejigantes carry blown cow bladders with which they make sounds and hit carnival attendees throughout the processions.

The traditional vigigante masks of the Ponce carnival are made of paper mâché and are characterized by the presence of multiple horns. The mask was developed by Ponce artisans in the early part of the 20th century.

They are made from newsprint paper mixed with homemade glue and paint. Sophisticated Ponce carnival masks are sought after by mask collectors and masks from Ponce have become a symbol of Puerto Rico at large.

The Carnival ends with the Burial of the Sardine, at which point everyone sings a song in Spanish that translates into: The burial of the Sardine event started in 1967.

The Ball Dance also started in 1967. The burial of the Sardine event also started in 1967.

As I said before, Juan Jose was too young to attend the Carnival. He begged his mother, Lupe, to let him go. He was very excited. Lupe made him a custom that scared everyone even Juan Jose.

It was a Sunday afternoon, when Juan Jose got all dressed up to go to La Plaza with his friend. Lupe wasn't feeling so happy to let Juan Jose go to la Plaza.

Juan Jose was too eager to let anyone stop him. He told his mother that he was going to be careful.

The problem was that at the plaza a lot of crazy people were getting drunk and throwing heavy object at the young adults that were really celebrating with colorful custom and holding their vegigas.

Let me tell you that Juan Jose was hit very badly and taken to the hospital. He never recovered from those severe injuries.

At the present time, there are no young children present at the carnival. Before joining the big celebration, everyone that is going to be part of the parade of the Vijigantes must fill out a form so that authorities have full control of the festival.

Every February, I go to see the parade. It is our tradition. I was born in Ponce and to me it is important to keep our traditions alive....

Chapter 2

The Ponceño Carnival

The Ponceño Carnival is the oldest in Puerto Rico. It is 250 years! This celebration continues to fill the streets of Ponce with history and tradition, bringing thousands to congregate along the route to admire the floats, school bands, queens and vejigantes that fill with color the multitudinous party that takes place before the beginning of Lent.

Have you ever wondered how these centennial celebrations originated or from whom we inherit?

To try to answer these and other questions, let's explore some curiosities and facts about Ponce's Carnival: El Carnaval Ponceño.

Carnival's roots are found in pagan traditions from ancient Egypt, where a festival was held at the beginning of spring to mark the end of winter.

This tradition reached ancient Greece when Alexander the Great conquered Egypt. Likewise, the Romans copied the festival from the Greeks and called it bacchanal in honor of the god of wine, celebrating it with excessive wine, dance, and music.

Little by little the tradition continued to expand throughout Europe, to later adopt a Christian meaning which they called carnival, an expression derived from the Latin phrase "carne" meat and "vale" goodbye, meaning goodbye to meat.

Since then, the carnival starts the Catholic fast of Lent and the consequent abstinence from meat.

The Ponce Carnival in its beginnings was a copy of the carnival that was celebrated in France. It became part of the local culture with the colonization of Spain.

In that Iberian country, the celebration of carnivals was important in cities such as Valencia, Seville, Barcelona, and Madrid.

Back in the island, at first what eventually became the Ponce Carnival, consisted of the celebration of luxurious, masked dances and it is believed that this tradition anchored in Ponce through immigrants from Catalonia and other regions who arrived at the Port of Ponce.

The agreement among historians is that the first carnival in Ponce was documented on a Tuesday in February 1858. It was the first masked ball held and a local business located on the corner where Villa and Concordia de Ponce streets intersect today.

In that property of Don Benito La Guardia, the masquerade ball was held in the pre-Lenten period, forever fixing the celebration of Carnival just before the beginning of Lent.

For this reason, this year we celebrate the 165th edition of the Ponceño Carnival in Ponce.

In its beginnings, the carnival exploited everything twisted and ordinary in everyday life. It began with the arrival of King Momo, represented by a person from the town and, as a mockery, the people unloaded all their hostility against him, throwing damaged eggs, flour, rotten fruit, and anything that could denigrate the king's appearance.

All this took place in the form of a "comparsa", to the sound of traditional music, where the participants paraded mostly masked or made up exaggeratedly. It was also normal for men to dress up as women and vice versa.

King Momo, Rey Momo, is a typical carnival character who introduces to a god from Greek mythology with the same name, Momo, who was the god of mockery, sarcasm, and madness.

In the Ponceño Carnival he is a celebrated person from the town who wears a gigantic mask made of papier-mâché and remains masked, without revealing her identity, until the end of the celebration, just before Ash Wednesday.

During that last night of celebrations, the "Burial of the Sardine," El Entierro de la Sardina, is also celebrated: a ritual in which a mock funeral is held with queens and people in chorus crying over the death of the sardine.

In local tradition, one version suggests that the sardine is the one who symbolically saves King Momo, who, in turn, in the old Spanish tradition, is sentenced to death at the end of the Carnival.

Other versions suggest that the burial of the sardine mentions the end of the festival and is considered the last mischief of the vejigantes, who hide the fish to make the blessed sin in Lent that is about to begin.

The Vejigantes are figures with demonic features that walk the streets of Ponce alone or in "comparsas", dressed in masks and costumes created by hand, usually carry inflated cow bladders in their hands with which they prowl among people, doing mischief.

Regarding the origins of his mask made of papier-mâché, it is mentioned that this traditional native mask from Ponce was born for the carnival from the integration of the concepts of the Franco-Spanish, Taino, and African mask.

It is also said that its origin is in the Playa de Ponce neighborhood, where the cattle slaughterhouse was located, from which horns were extracted for the vejigantes masks.

As well as the site to collect the bladders of the cows to inflate and paint in bright colors, to later use them to hit other people. Hence the name vejigante, "veji" from the word vejiga or bladder, and "gante" from the world gigante or giants, meaning giants with bladders.

This mask is so important and impressive, considered collectors' items and currently exhibited in museums and private collections throughout the world.

An important part of the carnival celebration in Ponce is the creation of commemorative posters. There are over 50 posters recording carnival memories.

The oldest found dates back to 1939! An interesting fact about these posters is that the first time we see an image of the vejigante monster is in 1964.

An important function of these posters is that, in addition to sharing information about the carnival's dates, they provide a sample of the essence of carnival or what was experienced that year.

For example, in the official poster of the Ponceño Carnival number 163, created by the artists of the Salón Boricua creative workshop, you can see the characters of the celebration coming out of an iPhone, alluding to the special edition of a virtual carnival, popularized by Facebook Live, something that marked what the city and the world experienced due to the Covid-19 pandemic.

This year the poster focuses on the Centennial Municipal Band and the Parque de Bombas, to whom the festivities are dedicated.

The 165th edition of the Ponceño Carnival is dedicated to one of the most important institutions of Ponce: La Banda Municipal de Ponce, which will celebrate its 140th anniversary of exemplary trajectory next September 2023.

Originally called La Banda de Bomberos or Firefighters Band, it was created by Juan Morel Campos when the musician and composer was 26 years old, in September 1883.

This was after the reorganization of the Firefighters Corps, which was founded in 1853, and which at that time was established in what had been the Pavilion of the Exhibition Fair of 1882, the same space that we have known since then as the Parque de Bombas.

After the early death of Morel Campos, Domingo Cruz "Cocolía," the great musician, composer, euphonium player and friend of Morel, carried on the legacy and directed the Banda de Bomberos de Ponce, ensuring that this tradition would be passed on to future generations.

Today, the "Centenaria Banda Municipal de Ponce" is the oldest and continuously performing band in the Caribbean, and the fourth oldest band in the world!

Why Ponce is Ponce? It is a town full of history and, I am proud to say, that I was born in Ponce. "Soy Ponceña con mucho orgullo."

Chapter 3

Covering the Ponce Carnival

Alice couldn't stand the man! How much more was she supposed to take? He was constantly late. Half the time he forgot his equipment. The rest of the time he was too busy checking himself in the mirror or flirting with her female staff to do his job properly.

Today was the absolute worst. He'd shown up to work with a poorly dressed with two women, one in each arm. Not to mention that he was over half an hour late.

They were in Ponce to cover the Carnival and most of her crew had enjoyed the festival. Even she'd even gone out last night and walked around, enjoying the sights, sounds, and food. Who wouldn't want to?

Seeing the two women plastering their naked bodies all over him this morning did something to her. David Smith had only been working on her crew for three weeks. He'd been hired by her boss, Antonio, and when she'd complained about him, Antonio had just smirked and told her it was out of his hands. What did that even mean?

She'd had a problem with David the minute she'd met him. He'd seemed so self-absorbed and huge. The man had arms the size of elephant trunks, and his neck was as thick as her thighs. Alice had known many men like him; self-absorbed, every one of them.

He probably spent more time at a gym than he did watching the news or learning about what was going on in the world. You needed to be up on current events if you wanted to stay working for one of the top media outlets.

Of course, the man was just behind the camera. She supposed the extra muscles came in handy when it came time to lug all that heavy equipment around.

Her last cameramen, Alberto, had been a short, frail-looking older man. She and the two other guys in her four-man crew, Joe, and Mark, had always had to help him unload the equipment.

As Alice, Joe, and Mark stood around waiting for David, she decided what needed to be done. When they made it back to Austin, she was going to make it her mission to see that David get his pink slip.

It wasn't as if she was a dictator. She'd even bought the whole crew drinks their first night in Ponce. She tried to enjoy herself around the three men. Joe and Mark had been on her crew for a few years, and she felt somewhat comfortable around them, however, with David there, she just couldn't seem to loosen up.

She thought he was very attractive, so maybe that had a lot to do with it.

Sexual tension was always a good reason to be nervous around someone. With him, it was more. She couldn't explain it, but it was almost as if he went out of his way to make her angry.

That first night, he only drank one beer and the rest of the evening had just sat around flirting with any woman that walked by, which happened to be a lot of women.

He flirted with everyone except her. Maybe that was it. She was used to getting hit on by coworkers, especially attractive ones. David went out of his way not to hit on her, which made her believe that he had something against her or that he was flirting with other women to see her reaction.

Whatever it was, she wasn't buying his act. At least she thought it was an act.

Now as he approached the van, he had a wicked smile plastered on his face.

She crossed her arms and grinned back, thinking about getting him fired.

"Sorry I'm late, boss. I found these two and we got to talking." She watched as the women blushed.

Yeah, I bet they were just talking, Alice thought.

"We had to carry all your gear out here ourselves. You owe Joe and Mark an apology."

He walked over and gave Mark a high five. One of the women walked over and gave Joe a kiss on his cheek, making the older man blush.

She realized that they were pretty much ignoring her, and she felt like she was just being a nagging woman.

They'd been in Ponce for over a week covering the festivals, and she'd had enough of all three of them.

Somehow David had gotten closer to Mark and Joe in the last week than she had in the last three years, which made her feel extremely annoyed and hurt.

As everyone piled in the van, she watched as the two young women trying to get in. She held her arm over the door and blocked them, looking over to David.

"They can't come along." She had yet to understand his expressions; his hazel eyes hid his emotions too well. Right now, she assumed he was annoyed. "She's right, girls," he said. She heard the standard frowning objections from both women who turned and kissed him one after another, then walked away.

Finally, they got in the van and headed out. Now they were late for the meeting with her source, whom she hadn't told her crew about.

Everyone was still under the impression that they were meeting Carmen Rodriguez, this year's Carnival Queen.

"Where did you say this meeting was?" Joe asked as he drove the narrow side streets. Alice gave him directions and once the van started climbing the hills towards the slums, everyone got very quiet.

Finally, Mark leaned forward and asked, "Alice, are you going to tell us why we are meeting the queen of the carnival up here in the slums?"

"We aren't." She sat forward in her seat as she felt the thrill and excitement of disobeying her boss set in.

"What exactly are we doing up here, then?" Joe asked, while keeping his eyes on the ever-narrowing streets.

"We are meeting a man about a job." She knew she was being vague, but she didn't want anyone to chicken out. Especially since she knew the story could earn her world recognition, and possibly even the Pulitzer.

"Tell me this isn't another scheme to get a Pulitzer." Joe looked over at her.

She waited to answer them until they pulled in front of a small, brightly colored yellow building.

Laundry hung from wires and ropes across the entrance of the alleyway. There were brightly colored designs on the houses that she knew marked each house and its occupant's loyalties to a particular drug lord.

Hector, her source, was standing in the doorway, looking a little nervous.

She'd met him late last night while she'd been enjoying the carnival. She'd just stepped out after dealing with David when a large man had approached her. He was an older man and at first, he'd scared her, since he'd approached her from behind.

He'd tried to pull her into the alleyway by her arm, and when she'd resisted, he'd told her that he knew she was a journalist, that he'd been watching her at her hotel as she covered the carnival.

At first, she'd shivered, thinking that someone had followed her, watching her. Then he'd gone into quick detail about what he did and who he worked for. David had stepped out of the hotel and had started walking towards them, so she'd arranged to meet him today.

He'd pushed a piece of paper into her hand with the address and directions to the meeting after he'd told her the time. She'd asked if he would be willing to go on camera with his story, but he'd shaken his head and left quickly as David had approached her. He'd acted like she'd been in trouble, but she just laughed at him and tried to have a good time getting lost in the crowd.

She didn't know why Hector wanted the interview. She was sure he must have been marked for death already for him to take such a bold step.

"Hector, I'm sorry we're late." She glared in David's direction. "We can be set up in under five minutes."

"I'm sorry, miss, I thought you were coming alone. I've changed my mind about talking to you." The man's eyes were darting in every direction, taking in her crew. She noticed his hands shaking and realized she had to do something quickly or she was going to lose the interview.

"Hector, why don't you and I go inside and talk."

It took her the whole five minutes that her crew was setting up to calm him down and convince him that he'd be perfectly safe. There was no way anyone would know it was him on the camera.

As the interview got started, she pulled out the list of questions she'd worked up earlier that morning. She knew how to work in an interview. She started with some easy questions to make him feel relaxed, then she built up to some harder questions, and finally she asked the doozy of all questions.

Hector was true to his word. He answered every question about his boss and his ties to the police, giving her details on how much money was involved. Most importantly, he had information on the connections between his boss, the police, and a local politician.

This was the scoop she was digging for. A chamber deputy, a judiciary, and a Supreme Court justice were all in the pockets of one or more drug lords, or worse, they were the ones in control.

Hector didn't have that last piece of information that would have tied it all up nicely.

When he talked about the connections, he stuttered and became very agitated.

Alice could tell he knew more, but before she could get names and more details, Joe pulled her aside.

"Alice, we need to leave. I think you have enough," he said. "Can I talk to you?" He motioned towards the doorway.

She looked at him for a few seconds, then followed him out front. "I'll be right back, Hector."

The man nodded and looked even more afraid. The second she stepped out the small opening, Joe turned on her.

"How dare you!" His face was red, and she noticed sweat running down his neck. She'd never seen him look so upset.

"How dare you put your crew at risk like this. I mean, we come down here, flashing our press badges all over the place. Then you get wind of this." He motioned towards the small box of a home.

"You didn't even bring your crew in on the secret. Just plow right through, as if you're the queen of TV. Did you think of our safety? Or that of the man in there, beyond this interview? I mean, look around!" He motioned to the courtyard. Their large white van sat in front of the row of huts that were falling, a white sign in a sea of trash.

"You may have covered his face, but can you cover the fact that now everyone within a one-mile radius knows that the man sitting inside talked to the press?"

She smiled, "Relax, Joe. This isn't his place. You see that symbol there?"

She pointed to the small patch of bright colors.

When Joe nodded, she continued, "That's the sign of the Red Command.

Earlier this year the police seized control of this whole area. They are in control here, not the drug lords."

She crossed her arms as she watched Joe look around and notice the small children playing in the streets. There were women and old men sitting outside, like they were enjoying a day at the beach.

You wouldn't see that if the drug lords still controlled this section. Smiling, she walked back into the room only to find David and Mark sitting in the darkened room alone.

"Where is Hector?"

David shrugged his shoulders and continued to play with his camera. Mark pointed to a doorway. "He said he needed a bathroom break."

Alice rushed towards the opening and realized it was a back door. "Great!

Can't you two keep your eyes on someone for five minutes?" She turned and glared at the men.

"Well, I guess the interview is over now, anyway," she said to Joe who had just walked in. "Pack it up, boys." She chewed her bottom lip, hoping she had gotten enough in the interview.

It seemed to take longer to get back down the hill to their hotel. The carnival was in full swing since it was the next to last evening. She wanted to work with Mark and get everything edited and send it to Austin before sundown. The two of them sat in the hot van and worked for almost three hours.

Finally, just before the sun set, when she was fully satisfied with the outcome, she grabbed the burned DVD of the footage and started back up to her room to call her boss.

She was halfway down the hall when David came rushing out of Joe's room. He grabbed her arm and pulled her into what appeared to be a closet.

"What?" She couldn't get another word out, as his big hand clamped over her mouth.

15

His muscular arms held her tight and the look in his eyes told her she'd better stay quiet. Then she heard loud noises. They seemed to go on forever. David pulled her down past a few shelves until, finally, they crouched on the floor behind a large row of toilet paper and towels.

His full weight was on her, crushing her to the hard ground. His hand was still over her mouth, blocking out any protest she had.

Then there was an explosion and she watched in horror as the door was ripped off the hinges. A large fire ball came rushing towards them. She tried to scream just before a large chuck of wood hit her head and everything went black.

Chapter 4

David and Alice

David fought to stay conscious by breathing slowly and blinking his eyes a few times. He'd been hit by a large chunk of wood from the door during the explosion.

He felt the slickness of blood oozing down the back of his head, and when he reached back, his hand came away red. He felt Alice's unconscious body under his and when he moved to sit up, he felt a wave of dizziness hit him. He continued to breathe slowly.

He knew they needed to get moving. Shaking his head lightly, he demanded that his body starts functioning. He looked down at Alice and noticed a large knot on her forehead.

Gently he pushed her bright brown hair aside to take stock of the wound. She might have a concussion. Running his hands over her, he felt for any broken bones or other lesions.

"Get your hands off me," she moaned as she tried to push his hands away.

He smiled. Good, she was alive and awake.

"We need to get out of here. The place is on fire." He watched as her eyes slid open. She was glaring at him. God, he loved it when she glared. He knew she couldn't stand him. He'd made a point to be as annoying around her as possible.

After all, it was all part of his character. David Smith was a self-absorbed, macho, chauvinist kind of guy, or so he'd thought when he'd created the persona. For the last two weeks it had been killing him to be around her.

She was bossy, egotistical, and very good at her job, not to mention sexy as hell.

He looked down at her now and realized some of her hair had been burned off and it was standing up in spots.

Her clothes, a white button-up and dark dress pants, were no longer recognizable and were black with holes all over them. He saw a couple of scratches on her and noticed they were bleeding. No doubt he had a few himself. He looked down and sure enough, his cargo pants and t-shirt were both riddled with holes.

"Alice, we have to get out of here." She moaned and sat up with her back against the wall.

"What was that?" She reached up and touched her forehead where the bump was and cringed at the pain. The smoke started getting thicker and he knew they needed to leave now.

"That was your drug lords telling us they don't like you poking your nose in their business."

"Don't be ridiculous." He watched in amusement as she tried to dust off her pants. He saw that she was missing a shoe, and when she noticed, she started looking around for it. He grabbed her hand and tried to pull her to her feet.

"Stop, I have to find it." She pulled her hand free and continued looking through the rubble that was all that was left of the linen closet.

The smoke was so bad, he was having a hard time looking down the hallway. He looked back at her. She was still on her hands and knees, searching for her shoe. He wanted to laugh.

"Alice, the hotel is on fire. We must get out of here. Leave your damn shoe." He tried to grab her arm again, but she just pulled it free again.

"I'm not looking for my shoe, you idiot! I'm looking for the DVD." She continued to rummage through the wreckage.

Seeing the black case that held the disk by the doorway, he bent and picked it up and stuffed it in the side pocket of his khakis. Then he walked over and picked her up and threw her over his shoulder, fireman style.

She screamed and kicked at him the entire hike down the flight of stairs to the main floor. Here there was a lot less smoke and when they got outside, he stopped and looked around.

People were rushing from the building, coughing, and screaming. Some had injuries, others just looked shaken.

Across the road sat their van, riddled with bullet holes. Mark lay on the ground outside, blood covering every inch of his body. Trying to keep her eyes pointed in the other direction, he started walking with her still flung over his shoulders.

They needed to get as far away from the hotel as possible. He headed in the direction of the carnival, hoping that if there was anyone watching for them to leave the hotel, he would lose them in the crowd.

He knew she'd seen the van and Mark when she stopped kicking and fighting him. She'd gasped and gone very limp. He hoped she hadn't passed out, but thought it might be easier on her if she had.

"You can put me down, now," she said softly.

He looked around and noticed several men following them. The hotel was three blocks away and the men were only half a block away from them.

"Sorry, Princess. We need to cover some ground quickly. I think it would be better if I drove for a while."

He picked up his pace and when he looked over his shoulder, he noticed the men had as well. Now he spotted five of them running after them. Damn, they were still a dozen or so blocks from the celebrations, and there was no way he could outrun them like this.

"How fast can you run? "David wasn't winded, but the blow to the back of his head was causing him to almost see double. What he needed was some sleep and some aspirin.

"Why?" she said between grunts caused by bouncing up and down over his Shoulder.

"Look behind us and tell me how many men you see chasing us."

He felt her hands on his back as she arched up and looked. Then he heard a gasp and he could tell that she had finally realized they were screwed.

"David, let me down. We'll be faster than what we're doing now."

"Stay with me. I mean it, Alice.

No matter what!"

He didn't even break his stride as he set her down on the ground. Then he had her hand in his hand as they raced down the hill towards the crowded streets. She was right, she was fast, and they plunged into the crowd a good block ahead of the five men.

Looking around as they entered the crowd, he realized they still stood out.

He'd been able to follow her in the crowd the other night easily by following her bright blond head. She hadn't even known he was following her. He'd been able to blend into the crowd very easily. Looking at her now, he knew this was going to be a problem again.

He stopped and taking her shoulders, turned her towards him. Then in one quick movement he ripped her tattered shirt off her as she squealed. The crowds around them cheered.

"What?" She tried to cover herself. Long strings of beads were thrown in their direction by the masses, and he quickly gathered a handful up. He placed them over her head, to make her look more festive.

Then he knelt in front of her and took her tattered pants in his hands, ripped each leg up high on her thigh, exposing her soft skin. He could see small cuts and bruises forming on her perfect legs, but in the dark, most would go unnoticed by the crowd. He removed her last shoe, so she stood on the street barefooted.

Then he quickly ripped his own torn shirt off, to the cheers from all the women around him. More beads were thrown and even a few bras. He smiled and looked at Alice who was gaping at his chest.

He assessed her and realized that her hair was the only problem left. She had long, bright brown hair, the kind that took conditioned every week. It was a beacon in a sea of darker heads.

Looking around, he found a woman with a large headdress of bright flowers and feathers. He grabbed Alice's hand and started towards her.

When they reached the woman, he smiled as he approached her. Two minutes later, they were making their way through the crowd, eating up as much distance as they could.

It took a while for them to push their way through the partygoers. Most were dancing but were drunk enough to try to touch them as they walked by. He could smell all the alcohol around him.

It was on everyone's breath as they passed by. That and the smells of cooked food surrounded them. He looked back to make sure Alice was right beside him, so he didn't lose her.

Even though her hand was locked in his, he just needed to see for himself that she was there. Several times they were surrounded by people and had to push their way out through the crowds.

Finally, they made it to a place where the crowd was thinning out. Alice quietly walked behind him, not putting up much of a fight. He looked back at her and smiled.

The purple headdress covered her bright head, and with her bra and very short shorts, she looked like a real party goer. At least until you noticed the frown and the tears slipping silently from her eyes. He'd have to deal with those later. Right now, he needed to get them to safety, and he knew just the place to go.

All they needed was some luck. He kept his eyes peeled for anyone that looked out of sorts in the crowd. This was hard in a sea of heads and faces. He knew they still had a dozen or so more blocks to walk and hoped that the crowd would stay thick enough that they could hide in the ocean of people the entire way.

He watched silently from the crowd as they disappeared into the masses. How could he lose sight of her so quickly? She'd been an easy target to follow the first night he'd been here. The fact that he had a dozen men out looking for her assured him that she'd be easily found by the morning.

There was no place she could hide for too long. She didn't know anyone here and there wasn't a place that would take her in that he didn't have eyes or ears on.

He wanted this all tied up nice and clean by the time he had to go back to the States tomorrow afternoon.

He couldn't afford to be out of sight for too long. He needed to be seen, to be in the public eye, where he belonged. He spotted one of his men across the crowd and watched as the man crossed the crowd to meet him.

"Have you spotted her?"

"No. Somehow, I lost them after they entered the street. We'll find her; she couldn't have gotten that far."

They were supposed to have her in their hands before the explosion ripped through the hotel, but when they'd arrived at the van, she hadn't been there. She must have gone into the building without the scouts seeing her.

He'd watched from across the street as the cameraman, David, had carried her out. At first, he'd thought everything was over, that she was dead.

He'd breathed a sigh of relief when he'd seen her move.

There was no way his boss would have let him live if she'd been dead. Even if the old man was going to kill her later, he'd been told to deliver her alive.

The crowd was nothing but a nuisance to him. The screaming, dancing fools bounced around him dressed in little to nothing, drinking like there was no tomorrow. They were making it hard for him to do his job. The job had been so simple, and yet his men had let her slip out of his grasp. He knew he needed to deliver Alice to his boss or he would have his head. He wanted his hands on her first.

His boss never told him she had to be untouched when he delivered her.

This was his last night in Ponce, and he needed to find her quickly, or he'd have to wait and let his men do all the work.

"Tell the men to look harder. They can bring in anyone they need. I'll double the price to whoever brings her to me tonight."

The man's eyes got large, and he hurried off, no doubt to relay the message to the other men he was paying.

Now all he had to do was go back to his hotel room and wait for her to be brought to him. Then he could finally get his hands on the beautiful Ann, before he turned her over and got his reward.

Alice was feeling lightheaded. Not only had she lost the disk that had caused all this mess, now Mark was dead and Joe. She realized she didn't know what had happened to Joe.

David had been pulling her along for over an hour in the crowd and she was sure he must be lost. After all, the man was a flake.

The loud music and the cheers from the crowd did little to clear the pounding in her head. The bottom of her feet hurt due to the lack of shoes. When she looked down, she realized her feet were completely black, and the nail polish on her toes had chipped off.

The stupid headdress he'd plopped on her head for some reason weighed a ton and she wanted to yank it off. Her body was hurting, her muscles were sore, and she had dried blood all over her. She was complaining in her mind, but she made a point to keep her mouth shut and not do it out loud. After all, Mark was dead.

Finally, what seemed like hours later, David pulled her into a small building out of the crowd. The tears had stopped, and she was starting to shake as the cooler air hit her.

Since her clothes were all gone, she felt the night chill on her exposed skin. The cuts and bruises just added to her discomfort. They walked down a long, dark hallway and when they reached the end, he knocked on the door and stood back.

His feet were braced wide apart, and he looked like he was preparing himself for a fight.

It took a minute before she heard someone on the other side of the door, possibly someone looking through the small hole at them. Then the door flew open, and a large black fist reached out and hit David square in the face. David did nothing to block or dodge the giant fist.

Alice couldn't help it, she squealed and tried to pull David away from the next blow, which landed on his jaw again, causing his head to snap back.

"I gave you the first two, but after that, I may just have to hit you back," David growled out.

Alice looked and saw the man attached to the fist. He was almost as impressive as David. His shoulders and arms were as thick, but he was almost a foot shorter and looked about ten years older.

"Damn boy, I told you if I ever saw your ugly face again, that would happen," Jaime said in a thick Spanish accent. Then the men shocked Alice by grabbing each other in a man-hug as blood trickled down from David's nose.

Half an hour later, Alice sat in an oversized chair with the god-awful head dress sitting next to her on the floor. She drank hot tea with a blanket wrapped tightly around her, as she listened to David and Jaime talking.

She was totally confused as to why the man was calling him Ivan instead of David. Her head hurt and her vision was starting to go gray. Before she realized it, she was being shaken awake, and David was looking down at her.

She was lying on the soft couch, and she'd been covered by a blanket. Then she realized that David was fully dressed in clean clothes, and it looked like he'd just showered.

She sat up and shook her head clear. "Where is Ivan?"

"He took off. He's going to let us stay until tonight. We have some things we need to take care of before we leave. I hope it's okay, but I left some stuff in the bathroom, through there," he said, pointing to a door at the end of a small hallway.

"I need you to take care of everything, shower, change into the clothes I left you. I'll make us some breakfast. Then once everything is ready and Ivan reports back, we can leave."

She looked towards the small window near the back of the room and realized the sun was already up. When she moved to stand, her head twisted a little.

David's hand rushed out to steady her as he pulled her closer.

She smelled the soap on his skin and felt his body heat through the beads she was still wearing. Then she remembered that that was pretty much all she was wearing and pushed his arms away.

"Why did that man call you David?"

He smiled at her and said, "Because it's my name. Take a shower, Princess, then I'll explain everything." He turned and walked into the small kitchenette without another word.

She watched his back and missed seeing the naked muscles that she'd followed for most of the night. She'd gotten used to seeing them and had even, at one point on their long hike last night, wished she could get up and feel them, wondering how they would feel under her hands.

Walking down the hall, she stepped into the small bathroom and leaned against the door. How could she be thinking of him like that? He'd been a thorn in her side for weeks. She was going to get him fired when she made it back to Austin.

Shaking her head, she noticed a small box on the countertop sitting next to a bag of clothing. Grabbing it up, she marched back into the other room.

"Is this some kind of joke?" She shook the box in front of his face. He held a spatula in one hand and a pan of sizzling eggs in another.

"No, Princess. It's not. Now go on and get ready."

"I am NOT coloring my hair..." she looked at the box and then shook it again, "...black!"

"Sorry, that's the only color Ivan had. He says he uses it to hide his gray."

David laughed and turned his back on her again as he placed a few slices of ham in another pan. The smell was wonderful, and Alice felt her stomach growling.

She felt like throwing the box at the back of his head. Then she noticed a large cut and a fresh line of blood coming from the base of his skull. She dropped the box and reached for his head.

"You're bleeding, you fool.

Didn't you take care of this?" She stepped closer and saw a large chunk of wood sticking out of his skin. "You have a chunk of wood in there." She took his head and tried to turn it towards the light. He didn't move.

"I'm fine, Princess. Just go get ready."

"No, I'm not moving until I clean out this wound." She crossed her arms and glared at him.

He was a fool. Didn't he know that injuries like that could become infected?

"If I let you clean it up, will you color your hair and get cleaned up?"

She thought about it, "Why do I have to color my hair?"

"Because this blond," he reached out and ran a lock of her hair between his fingers, "sticks out in a crowd and we need to blend in. Plus, whoever is after us, is looking for a blond woman. This might throw them off our trail until we can get out of Ponce."

She tilted her head and thought about it. He did have a point.

"Yes, fine. Now come into the light so I can get the wood out."

She pulled out a chair at the small table near the window and motioned for him to sit. He took his time removing the pans from the heat, then wiped his hands. He walked over with a towel and a bottle of alcohol, then sat with his back to her.

She was reminded of following him last night and the gentleness in which he'd talked to her as they made their way through the crowd. His hand had always clasped hers tightly, almost as if he was very concerned, he'd lose her.

As she started to pull the wood from his skin, she asked, "Do you think Joe made it out of the hotel?"

He was quiet, too quiet. She stopped what she was doing and walked around to look him in the eyes.

"David ? Did Joe make it out?" She saw the answer in his eyes. "What…how…?"

"Before I found you, I walked into our room, and he was there. I think they'd gotten to him first before shooting up the van and Mark.

They must have left a bomb in the room with him. Maybe they hoped to get us with it." She closed her eyes and thought of Joe's two daughters. He was seventeen and a fifteen-year-old. Mark had been single, but that didn't stop her from mourning them both equally.

"I was stupid," she said, keeping her eyes closed on a wave of new tears.

She didn't realize that he'd stood up until she felt his arms on her shoulders.

"Alice" She opened her eyes and looked at him. She could tell he was struggling with the right words to say, and she knew that he thought she was to blame, as well.

Using the back of her hand, she dashed away from the tears and walked back behind the chair.

"Sit. I want shower and clothes." He sat and she got back to work getting the splinter out of his skull.

Then she went into the bathroom and used the box of color on her blond hair.

She'd had her hair many colors in the past, all variations of blond. This had been the lightest she'd gone and to be honest, it had been nothing but a pain since she'd bleached it.

She'd thought it would make her look better on camera, but it had only ended up washing out her skin tone. Plus, the upkeep was more than she wanted, not to mention how impossible it was to make it look shiny for the cameras. She had multiple bottles of oils she had to use just to keep her ends from breaking.

After twenty minutes with the dark color in her hair, she jumped in the shower and used the bottle of shampoo to wash all the dirt and blood from her body.

Her feet took longer to clean since she had dirt and dust in between her toes. Her pedicure was a complete loss. She hunted through the cupboards in the bathroom, but didn't find anything that resembled nail polish remover.

Finally, she looked at the bag of clothes and was happily surprised when she found a pair of khaki's, a white tank top, and a light tan button up shirt, not to mention a new bra and panties that were just her size. She started thinking about how he happened to have a change of clothes that fit her.

She assessed her reflection and was almost pleased at the image that stared back at her. Her long hair was a nice, rich shade of black which highlighted the lightness of her eyes somehow. The shirt and pants were a nice fit, accentuating her curves.

She was taller than most women at five nine, and her legs always looked extra-long and skinny. The downside to the height was her larger shoe size. She looked down at her still-bare feet and wondered what she was going to do. There hadn't any shoes in the bag.

Walking from the room she saw David sitting at the table with a small phone, frowning. She walked over and sat next to him.

"I guess I better call Austin." She looked at her hands on the table and wanted more than anything not to have to tell her boss that she'd killed Joe and Mark.

"I've already reported in," he said and scooped her a big spoon full of eggs.

She looked up at him and frowned. "What?"

Chapter 5

The Explosion

David watched her eyes blink several times. "Austin knows what happened. It's all over the news that we were killed in that explosion. I called them to set the record straight," he said and then started eating.

"Did....did you tell them about my meeting with Hector?" She twisted her hands in her lap, looking very nervous.

He shook his head no, and she relaxed a little in her seat. "I didn't see any reason to tell them what happened, other than we were alive.

"What did Anthony say?" She leaned closer to his chair.

"I didn't talk to Anthony. I talked to Darrell."

She gasped and started choking. He quickly slapped her back lightly a few times until she could breathe smoothly again.

"Easy, Princess. There's nothing to get worked up about."

She glared at him, "Would you stop calling me that. Besides, there is plenty to get worked up about. You talked to Darrell, the head of the network."

She quickly stood up and started pacing the floor. He watched her for a few seconds, then decided to go back to eating as she thought.

When he was almost done with his meal, she sat down next to him and took a small bite.

"What did Darrell say?"

He rolled his eyes and set his fork down. "He said to get our butts back to Austin as soon as possible. Which I intend on doing as soon as you finish your eggs."

She looked at him and he could tell he'd crossed the line. Her blue eyes showed signs of stress and lack of sleep. Not to mention the knot that was still on her forehead. It was the first real look he'd gotten of her since she'd come out of the restroom.

He'd been too occupied with shoveling in the fuel he knew they'd need for the journey they were going to have to make later.

The dark hair suited her, suited her very well. Her blue eyes looked lighter and more noticeable. When she talked, the dimples at either side of her mouth showed. The pants and shirt were a perfect fit, and he saw with some humor that she was still shoeless.

"I guess I'd better call everyone myself...my father...." He could see her mind whirling to what her family must think.

"Darrell said he'd call your father." He looked back down at his empty plate, trying to hide his lie. It had taken almost fifteen minutes for him to assure her father, his employer, that she was okay.

He thought he knew how she'd feel if she knew the whole truth. He needed her to cooperate with him and if she knew the whole truth, she might decide to try and make it back home by herself.

He knew there was no way she'd make it out of Ponce by herself, let alone all the way back to Austin out of Ponce.

He'd sent Ivan out on a hunt early this morning. He needed to know who was after them. Well, maybe not who, but at least how many men would be looking for them.

Ivan had been his right hand over the last eight years. David's security business didn't even have a name. He didn't need one. Word of mouth was the only way he was hired. High-powered accounts and high-powered clientele hunted him down to handle their risky security needs.

The first year he'd gone into business, he'd had more jobs than he could handle alone. So, a year after he'd retired from the government, he'd hunted down several of his closest buddies and hired them all. Now he was thinking of hiring more of his old friends to help.

This time around he had a plan, one he'd used several years back on another job. He knew it was most likely their best option for getting out of Ponce alive.

Roughing it had always been in his blood.

He'd spent countless summers as a child camping in the Pacific Northwest with his father. Then when he'd joined the forces, he'd spent even more time roughing it.

Looking over at Alice, he doubted she knew the true meaning of roughing it.

Although he had to admit that after last night, he had a little more respect for her.

Not once had she complained about her situation. She'd even walked the entire night barefooted and almost naked.

Sure, she'd questioned him, but he'd done nothing so far to earn her trust. So far all he'd shown her was that he was a self-absorbed, male chauvinist. He smiled thinking of how well he'd played his part.

Getting up from the table, he walked into the next room without a word.

When he came back, he had a pair of tan boots hanging by the shoestrings and a large black bag draped over his shoulder.

Tossing the shoes down next to her feet, he carried the bag over to the stove and started filling it with items from Ivan's cupboards, making sure to only grab what they could use.

His bag was already full of other items from Ivan's back room, items meant to keep them alive in the following days.

"Listen, Prince..." He stopped when she glared at him. "Listen, Alice. We have quite the journey ahead of us. It would be better to work together than against one another.

I know it's hard thinking about Joe and Mark. I'm just as sorry to know that they're both gone. We must think about ourselves for a while.

Getting back to the States is top priority and to do that, we will need to stay low. No phones, no credit cards, no buses, no planes, nothing.

We're going to be roughing it for a while, and I need you to keep the complaining to a minimal. Is that acceptable?"

He waited as her eyes flashed with anger.

"I don't complain. Besides, why can't we just hop on the next plane?"

He sat back down and felt his patience wearing thin.

"Did you forget the meeting with Hector yesterday? The men he used to work for have people in high places. High enough that the second we step foot in a public place and try to get out of Dodge...well, you can figure out the rest."

She quietly thought about it while eating the toast and eggs. "Is there any other way?" When he shook his head no, she asked, "What are your plans?"

He could tell she didn't trust him.

"We hike. We'll be out of Ponce by sunset and in the hills by nightfall. We travel as far as we can each day until we reach San Juan."

"San Juan? Isn't that north from here?" He nodded, and she continued, "How going north get us back to the States?"

"Because, Princess, they will be thinking we are heading south, and I have connections in San Juan that will take us to states. Until we get to San Juan, we are going to be traveling light. So, if there is anything you need, you'd better get it now. Ivan has a fully stocked room in the back."

He pointed towards the supply room. "Grab whatever you want and put it in the brown backpack on the floor. Pack light, you'll be carrying it all yourself."

She got up and started walking towards the door. "Oh, and Princess?"

He waited until she turned and glared at him before finishing. "Make sure you pack a blanket, rain poncho, and more socks. We'll be going through the jungle."

He watched her walk down the hall and disappear into the room, then he picked up his phone and dialed Ivan's cell.

"How's it looking out there?"

"Not so good. Your girl did a fine job of getting a lot of people pissed at her.

The word is she's quite the hot commodity."

"Yeah, I figured that. What do the paths look like?"

"Not so good. I think you'll be safe taking the route you have in mind. I can make sure to spread the word that I saw you heading south. Not too sure if the path will be completely cleared."

"Thanks, Ivan. We should be out of your place before you get back."

"No problems, man. Hey, David?"

"Yeah."

"I'm sorry I hit you the second time. I know you didn't deserve it."

He smiled. "Sure, I did." Then he hung up and went to see what Alice was packing in her bag.

Alice walked into the dark room and felt around for a light switch. When the room flooded with light, she gasped. It was full of tall shelves stocked with everything from flashlights to rubber hoses. She almost tripped over her backpack as she started walking the aisles. Why would Ivan have all this stuff?

Who was he? How did David know him?

Taking the bag, she started walking the aisles, grabbing a flashlight, grabbing a handful of batteries, a box of matches, and other basic items. When she reached the back, her bag was heavy with stuff she thought she'd need. She'd spent four years in the Brownies growing up and knew what it took to go camping.

She spotted a small silver box on the top shelf and took it down. Inside was a silver .45. She reached in and felt its weight, knowing she had to make room in her bag. She grabbed a box of bullets and before placing the gun in the small side pocket of the bag, she made sure it was unloaded.

Her father had forced her to take gun classes a few years back, so she knew how to handle a weapon, especially a .45. It was one of her favorites. Her mind flashed to an image of Mark's body. She closed her eyes to a wave of despair and guilt.

How could she have been so stupid? She shouldn't have taken the chance she had. She should have thought about what the consequences could be. She'd known ahead of time what she was going into with that interview.

She was thinking of going against the drug lords and the politicians, high-powered people who had run Ponce for years. Not only did they have power, but an unlimited supply of money.

She didn't think about her coworkers safety, she hadn't even thought about hers. She'd only been focused on the prize. The Pulitzer. The recognition. The fame.

She could kick herself now for her pride and stupidity. It was her fault, all her fault, and there was nothing she could think of to make it right. The despair was almost overwhelming. Looking around the room, she could just imagine herself sinking down and crumbling with hopelessness.

How would she ever recover from something like this? The guilt of her coworkers' lost lives would always weigh on her conscience. She wanted to bang her head against the wall. She wished she'd never survived the explosion.

It would have been easier on everyone.

Then she shook her head and cleared it from the dark thoughts. This wasn't her. She'd never once thought anything like that before. She blinked a few times and her mind whirled.

Survivor's guilt. She'd heard the term several times in the past. She had interviewed plenty of vets that had been diagnosed with PTSD. She knew that Post-Traumatic Stress Disorder could hit anyone, but never in her life did she think it could hit her or that it would be so weakening.

She'd been standing in the same spot for almost ten minutes, and in that time she'd gone from fear to depression, to thoughts of her own death, then back to acceptance.

So many emotions in such a short time. Then her mind focused on David, and she wondered how he was dealing with it all. Of course, he didn't have the extra guilt of causing everything. Was he having issues like she was?

One thing was for sure, she thought as she straightened her spine. When she walked out of this room, she was going to leave all those dark thoughts behind her. Her father had always taught her that whatever didn't kill her, only made her stronger.

She would never put a story in front of other's safety again. She should have been smart enough to begin with, but now she knew she'd never make the same mistake again.

She looked around to see if there was anything else she'd need in the room to help them survive the next few days.

As she started walking back out of the room, she spotted a small bottle and started laughing.

"What?" Nathan ducked his head in the door. "What's so funny?" He walked over to her.

"This." She held up the bottle. "Fingernail polish remover. Just what I needed."

She smiled at him and for the first time since meeting him, she saw him really smiling back.

Smiling changed him somehow. His whole face lit up and he became almost goofy looking. Gone was the self-absorbed, cocky attitude, the macho man who was full of himself.

Instead, there was this muscular man who reminded her more of a teddy bear. Looking at him smile made her want to smile even more.

"Listen, David"

"David," he said and took her bag from her hands.

"What?" She continued to look at him, and his smile was doing something to her insides.

"My real name is David Smith." He lifted the bag and nodded his head. "This shouldn't be too heavy for you to carry." He walked out of the room and set it next to his black one, which looked equally full.

She took the bottle of remover with her and followed him. "Your name is David Smith? You are David Smith?" When he nodded his head, she crossed her arms.

"Did my father send you?"

Chapter 6

Protecting Alice

David walked at a steady pace as he watched the back of Alice's dark head.

She defiantly fit in to the crowd now. Before, heads had turned when she walked down the street and men had seemed to fall aside with their tongues wagging.

At least that's what he always imagined. She had that effect on men, kind of like the coyote in the cartoons when steam shot out of its ears, and its eyes did the slot machine spin.

Okay, so it wasn't that bad. If he wanted to be totally honest, that's the way he'd felt when he'd first seen her. She'd walked across the room in a hot red outfit, and he'd lost control of his wits. Not only had his temperature risen, well… he shook his head and cleared the image from his mind.

They'd been walking for almost an hour and already he could tell she was slowing down. So far, they hadn't run into any trouble. When Alice stumbled, he reached out and took her arm.

She yanked it free and glared at him. He smiled at her in return, which only caused her to frown. The small crease between her eyebrows caused him to smile even more.

"Would you stop doing that?" She turned her head away from him. When he smiled, she felt her insides melt. He had a lopsided smile, and she could just make out a small dimple to the right side of his mouth, not to mention the small cleft in his chin.

It just screamed to be kissed, and it upset her that she was thinking along those lines. Especially since her two friends had just been killed.

"Fine, next time I'll let you fall on your pretty face."

He shrugged his shoulders.

"Not that!" She adjusted her backpack for the hundredth time.

"What then?"

"Smiling. You look like an idiot when you do it." She frowned at him again.

He couldn't help it; he laughed out loud. He was happy to see a small smile form on her lips.

"If the bag is too heavy, I can carry it," he said after she adjusted her bag again.

"It's not. I just didn't think we'd be marching at such high speeds."

He almost laughed again. "Princess, we haven't even begun to march. Wait until we hit the outskirts of town. I'm sure there will be plenty of men looking for us there and we may have to do some running."

He looked around and realized they were less than three blocks from the edge of the city. "We'd better eat lunch and rest here, just in case."

He walked over to a small shop and sat on the bench next to the doorway.

Here, on the outskirts of town, the walls and shops were covered with graffiti.

The buildings were crumbling, and the roads were used and old. There was trash everywhere, covered with the musty smell of mold and cooked food.

Alice walked over and sat next to him and watched as he removed a small brown bag from his pack.

"Here." He handed her a small baggie of cheese and crackers, then he took out one of the many sealed bags of beef jerky and handed it to her.

She sat and ate the food in silence. He'd expected her to complain about the food, or maybe her feet. Instead, she just watched people walking by and silently ate everything he'd given her.

Then, she pulled out a bottle of water and downed half the contents.

"Did my father send you?" she asked again. He'd gotten out of answering it before when Javan had come in. They'd left shortly after he'd reported everything he'd discovered.

David nodded his head and finished drinking his own water. Then he turned to her and noticed her frowning.

"If it helps, he didn't know this was going to happen."

"If he didn't think this was going to happen, then why did he hire you? What else is going on that I would need GI Joe to save me from?"

He smiled. "Is he still calling me that?"

Alice frowned even more. "The kid thinks you can walk on water."

David thought about it. Her half-brother, Blake, had been eight at the time he'd saved him, which made him around thirteen now.

"Is he chasing girls yet?" He smiled.

Alice laughed. He enjoyed the rich sound and the way her eyes lit up.

"He started two years back. He has quite a collection of girlfriends. He took two girls to a school dance a few months back."

As she continued to talk about her brother, David noticed how she relaxed and looked like she was enjoying herself. He could plainly see that she cared about her brother.

He remembered when he'd finally found his older half-sister, Ruth Ann.

She'd been stolen as a baby by her biological father and raised under the name of Roberta.

He'd run into her at the Brooklyn hospital a few years back while he was on a job.

When he had seen her, he'd done a double take. She looked so much like a younger version of his mother; he knew instantly that he had found his missing sister. He'd followed her and broken into her place just to confirm his intuition.

After being satisfied that she was Ruth, he'd left her a small clue he knew she could easily follow back to their mother. After all, he'd found out that she was a top New York detective at the time.

Roberta found the clue and less than a month later tracked his parents down, finally coming face-to-face with her real family. He'd attended her wedding to Ric Derby shortly after that and less than two year later had been at the baptism of their daughter, Rose.

"Are you listening to me?" Alice interrupted his thoughts.

"Yes. You said your stepmother Coleen had a field day after Blake was returned, and wouldn't let him leave the house for almost two months."

He smiled when she frowned back at him. He was thankful for his great memory, something he shared with his sister, Roberta. Maybe that's what made them both suited to do the jobs they were in.

Since getting married, Roberta had retired from the police force and was head of security for her husband's large art galleries, a move that had caused David to second guess his life.

He had retired from the military and gone into private practice for himself shortly afterwards.

Taking odd jobs here and there allowed him to have weeks, even months off so, he could spend more time with his family or just do some traveling, something he had always enjoyed.

"It should have been me."

"What should have?"

"In the van. I was just there. I had just left. If I had…"

"Stop!" He turned to her and took her shoulders into his hands.

"It's called survivor's remorse, Alice, and you're too smart to fall into the trap of what if's."

She looked at him as tears slid down her face. He wanted to gather her up and hold onto her, promising her that everything would be okay. The look on her face told him it was too soon. She didn't trust him, yet.

"I know. I understand it, but you can't deny the fact that I'm to blame. If I hadn't done the interview...."

He shook her shoulders lightly. "If I hadn't taken this job, you'd be lying in the gutter next to Mark."

The shocked look on her face told him that he was heading down the right path to snap her out of her guilt. He knew he was being harsh, but he needed her at full mental capacity.

He knew what was lying ahead, and he couldn't drag her physically or mentally the entire way through the jungle. She needed to take the steps and judging by the anger in her eyes now, she was on a fast track to recovery.

Looking around, he could see they had taken enough time. The next few hours would be a lot harder than the first half of the day. The steep hills and paths they were going to take were just plain torturous.

He'd had to use this pathway once before and could remember every sore muscles after the few days of hiking. He kept this information from Alice, thinking that if she knew ahead of time what he was about to subject her to, she'd change her mind about trusting him.

"We'd better get going." He stood and pulled her to her feet. He pulled her closer than he'd intended and enjoyed the spark of desire that crossed her face.

Interesting. He closed the distance between them by pulling her closer and noticed her eyes softening. Very interesting, he thought. Maybe the hike through the hills wouldn't be so bad after all.

"What?" He threw the glass across the room and watched as it shattered against the wall. "You promised me you'd have her by morning. I don't know if you know it, but it's after one. I leave in less than five hours. I don't care what you do or who you must hire.

Find that woman or you can forget about ever working in New York again."

He could feel the vein in his temple bulging as he looked across at the two men. He turned his attention to the larger man.

"I told you; I don't think the cameraman was who you said he was. He must be from some kind of military forces to have disappeared like that. Maybe he's an agent? All I know is that I have over a hundred men out looking, not to mention all the loyalists who have their eyes and ears out. Miss Rhodes has disappeared from Ponce."

He leaned over the table and looked at the man. Even though the man was bigger than he was, he wasn't afraid of him. After all, he was the one with all the power. If he didn't like how the man was doing his job, all it took was one word from him and he would see to it that he ended up floating downriver. Using his power and money always made him feel better.

What good was being second in command if you couldn't use the power occasionally? Of course, he wouldn't let anyone know that he was as easily replaced as anyone else.

He'd only been in this position for four years. He could still remember his predecessor. Seeing the man's head leave his shoulders in one clean blow from his boss's sword was an image he carried with him every day.

He liked to think it helped motivate him to be the best he could be. Knowing what would happen to you if you failed was always a great motivator. He used it with the men under him. After all, none of them had ever seen or met his boss. To say the man was a hermit would have been an understatement.

In the four years he'd worked for him, he'd only seen him faceto-face a handful of times.

"I don't care who the man is that she's with. It can't be that hard-to-find a single spoiled girl in this city, even if she is with an army of special agents.

If you don't find her by the time, I leave Ponce…"

He was done with threats. Pulling out his gun, he aimed it at the smaller man's chest and fired. He didn't even blink as the man hit the floor with a shocked look on his face.

The bigger man's face said it all. Maybe now he would get something done right.

He calmly set his gun back on the desk and sat down. "Now, clean up this mess and get back to work." He flipped open his laptop and got back to work, not paying any attention to the man carrying the body out.

He had an email to send and knew he wouldn't like the response. Alice was going to kill him. They were on hour five of their 'small trek', as he'd called it, and not only were her feet killing her, but she was also sure she'd sweat more fluids than she had taken in, or weighed, for that matter. He'd never told her they were going to be hiking through the jungle at top speeds.

If he had, she would have told him where to go and how to get there.

"David." She corrected herself. "I have to stop."

"Shhh!" He'd been acting strange for the last half a mile. She had a few rocks in her boots and needed a moment to use the nearest tree.

Her shirt was sticking to her skin, and she wanted nothing more than to remove it and toss it aside. The bugs were so bad under the canopy of the trees, she didn't want any new bites on exposed skin.

Looking at the back of his head, she realized he wasn't fighting any bugs off.

"David, I need to stop." She thought this name suited him. He turned and looked at her, his eyes burrowing into hers. She tried very hard not to look away. She knew when to stand her ground and this was one of those times.

They'd been walking for hours without so much as a complaint from her.

Normally she would pour out them, but considering her being at fault for their predicament, she bit her tongue.

He nodded and she relaxed, letting out the breath she'd been holding. She turned and started walking towards the nearest large tree.

"Where are you going?" he growled out.

She turned quickly and put her hands on her hips.

"If you don't mind, I'm going to go behind that tree and use the facilities. I'm sure I will be perfectly safe seeing as it's only ten feet away."

She turned and banged the rest of the way. Once behind the tree, she dropped her pack from her shoulders and almost fell over without the extra weight holding her down. Her shoulders were killing her. She leaned against the tree and closed her eyes as she rolled her head, using her hands to massage the sore muscles.

She bent over and stretched her back muscles and was about to stand up again when she heard a loud bang. She jumped and turned to see David standing there with his machete in one hand and a large snake the thickness of his thigh in the other.

Its large head was on the ground, and she watched in horror as he slowly untwisted its body from around his arm then dropped its limp body to the ground at her feet.

"Always check the tree before you stand under it for too long." He turned and walked away, leaving her staring at the large boa. She shivered then grabbed her pack up and followed him back to the small clearing.

"I thought you had to use the facilities?"

She could see him laughing at her but didn't care. Images of snakes, leopards, and all the other creepy or crawling things that lived in this jungle flashed in her mind.

Things that wanted to eat her. She shivered again and didn't even mind that his eyes were laughing at her.

"You forgot to put on your bug repellent." He walked over to her, took out a small tub from his pack and handed it to her.

"I am not wearing that stinky stuff." She crossed her arms and looked at the repellent she'd smelled earlier.

"You think that snake was bad? Try malaria or yellow fever. Put it on, Princess. The only person who can smell you is me, and I don't care what you smell like."

She took the tube and he turned to walk behind a large bush, no doubt to relieve himself. She slathered the thick cream on her exposed skin. She had over three dozen bites on her arms already and was trying very hard not to scratch them so they didn't scar up.

The thick cream stank, but when she rubbed it over her bites, she could feel the itching dissolve.

She still had to go to the bathroom, so after rubbing the cream into her arms, she went behind a small tree, and after spending several seconds looking up into the branches above her head, quickly dropped her pants.

When she walked back to where her pack was, she was happy to see David leaning against a tree, looking bored.

"How much farther are we going to go tonight? How can you tell you're going in the right direction?"

She sat on her pack and removed her left boot to empty it of the dirt and pebbles that had been bothering her for the last hour.

"I want to go another two hours before we make camp." He handed her a small pouch of beef jerky as he popped a piece into his mouth.

She didn't know if she would make it two more hours, but when she wanted to voice her complaints, an image of Mark popped into her head, and she closed her eyes.

"There was nothing you could have done," he said softly. She looked at him and realized he must have guessed where her thoughts had turned. She looked down at her boot and played with the laces.

"If I hadn't taken the chance, they would both still be alive." She didn't realize the tears were coming, but knew she'd held them at bay for over a day and that they had to come at some point.

"Alice." She saw his boots by her feet, but kept her eyes fixed on her own boot and hands.

"I know you think that you were foolish doing that interview, but what you were trying to do was a very noble thing. The world should know about the injustice going on down here.

Did you see those people in the streets?" He knelt and put his finger under her chin, bringing her eyes up to meet his.

"Those people live in fear every day that they're going to be killed for talking to the wrong person or for crossing the wrong street. The drug lords have complete control there and it just makes me angry to think that what Hector said might be true. That government officials may have control of it all. The people need to know."

His face was so close to her, she could see his hazel eyes. So close that, even though she was coated in bug repellent, she could no longer smell the stinky stuff.

Instead, all she could smell was him. He had a musky, sexy scent, and she wondered if he tasted as good as he looked. What would it be like to run her hands and mouth all over him? To play her fingers over the ripples in his arms and chest she'd seen the night before.

She felt his finger on her chin and enjoyed when he moved his hand and pushed a strand of her hair behind her ear. Then he ran his hand into her hair and pulled her closer so that he was a breath away.

"This is probably a mistake," he whispered right before he laid his lips gently on hers.

Yes, this was a mistake, she thought as his mouth moved over hers and she felt a shiver run down her spine. Her hands went into his dark hair, holding him closer as she tilted her head and took the kiss deeper.

She was probably still in shock from everything that had happened to her in the last day. After all, it was just yesterday she'd sworn she'd get him fired because he was an incompetent fool who didn't know how to do his job.

Now she realized he was doing his job and she was alive today because he'd been good at it. She felt him pull away and held off, opening her eyes for a few seconds. She could taste his lips and wanted more. Hell, if she could, she'd probably jump him right here and now. Then she opened her eyes and looked at him and realized things with him weren't going to be as easy as a quick fling.

They had a long trip ahead of them and their lives were in his hands. They didn't have time to stop and cruise in the forest.

Remember the snake? she asked herself and felt a shiver of disgust flow through her.

"I hope that wasn't because of my kiss." He smiled.

"Oh, no! That was for the snake."

When he smiled and made a point to look down at his crotch, she laughed. "Not that snake, the one who's head is lying a few feet from its body over there."

He laughed. "I know. I just love messing with you. Come on."

He stood and held out his hand to help her back up, but then realized she'd yet to put her boot back on.

"We'd better get moving again."

She dusted off her sock and slid on her boot, hating the feeling of the wetness from her sweaty sock, but knowing it wasn't as bad as it could have been.

An hour later she could have kicked herself for jinxing it. The rain wasn't just coming down, it was pouring down on them like someone was hovering overhead with an unlimited number of full buckets.

She tried to look up past her rain hat to see why the canopy of leaves above them wasn't sheltering a little of the water, but every time she tried, she got a face full of water. It was worse than standing under a broken showerhead.

David continued to march along at the same pace as he was unfazed by all the water. Their rain ponchos sheltered them from most of the damp, however her boots and the legs of her pants were muddy and soaked.

She didn't know how much longer she could tolerate hiking at this pace.

Every time she stepped down, she slid a little in the mud and had to make sure she didn't end up on her butt.

"David ?" She had to shout over the sound of the rain hitting the leaves. He continued to march without looking back. "David!" She pulled on his sleeve.

"Can we stop?"

He looked down at her and she hoped he saw the desperation in her eyes. She was tired, more tired than she'd been in years. The lack of a good night's sleep and the stress of everything that had happened in the last twenty-four hours had been slowly catching up with her.

What had finally caused the weariness to sink in was the downpour of the steady, cold rain.

"Can you walk five more minutes? There's a safe place up here where we can stop.

The rocks will shelter us from the rain, and we may even have a dry place to sleep for the night."

It sounded wonderful, so she nodded her head and they continued. Thoughts of a soft bed ran through her head, but she knew she'd be sleeping on the hard ground instead. She was glad she'd packed an extra blanket in her bag.

Even though it was in the upper eighties, she felt chilled and knew the second they stopped her blood would cool and she'd be cold. They took a rocky path that shot off the main pathway. It climbed high above a tall ridgeline. The sharpness was a little hard to maneuver with the slick mud underfoot and it took them twice as long as he'd hinted at to finally reach the top.

They had to hold onto tree branches and rocks to help them climb the last few steep feet. Once they made it, she almost felt like crying with relief.

When they reached the top, she understood why he'd pushed so hard to get here. The large moss-covered rocks crossed in a pattern and underneath was a perfect teepee-shaped cave with a small waterfall to the right.

The water rushed into a small pool that she assumed was normally very calm. Today, however, all the rain had caused the little lake to look like the ocean during a storm.

There were even little waves that lapped at the pebbled shoreline. They walked around the water's edge and made it into the stone archway, and she breathed a sigh of relief. It was hard to explain, but the steady pelting of the rain on her skin was almost annoying. She felt like it had sandblasted the top layer off.

Her feet hurt, her head hurt, and she knew she had a few new blisters. Setting her back down, she moved to sit when David grabbed her arm.

"Better wait until I check it out. Other animals like to take shelter from the rain."

She jumped up. How could she have forgotten they were in the jungle?

She picked her pack up and hugged it to her chest as pictures of spiders, snakes, and bats danced in her mind again.

David took out his flashlight and checked every corner of the small space.

"We're clear." He smiled when he saw the nervous look on her face.

"I don't like creepy-crawling things. Are you sure?"

He smiled and then ran his light around again. "Yes, we're clear."

She relaxed a little and set her bag down, then sat in the dry dirt, happy to be off her feet.

Chapter 7

A Dangerous Situation

David watched Alice across the small space as she slept. He'd sat across from her last night at Javan's and watched her, much like he was doing now. She slept like he'd dreamed of doing for years, like the whole world had dropped off and she had no cares.

He knew the hike had been hard on her. Hell, it had been hard on him, but he was used to being uncomfortable and tired. He'd done it all his adult life and had no plans of letting up any time soon. He liked his job and the travel.

He liked helping people out and working with his buddies from his time in the corps. He was very glad that he and Ivan had patched up their relationship. He'd been his best friend for so many years.

David had hated knowing the man was not around to call when he got in a tight spot. Above everything else about the job, David liked the danger and the thrills he got when he outmaneuvered his opponents.

It was like a game to him. He'd always been good at it. When he was a kid, he'd played paintball wars with all his friends. He'd always won. His high school buddies hadn't realized the game wasn't about shooting but about strategy, something he was good at.

David tried to close his eyes while keeping on alert. He felt his muscles relax one at a time until finally he could focus on the sounds around him, listening for anything out of the ordinary. He could hear only the gentle rain hitting the stones, the rushing sounds of the waterfall, and Alice's light breathing.

Listening to Alice breathe, made his mind switch from protection mode to thinking.

As he slept, he dreamed about how soft her skin would feel, how her lips had felt against his. He remembered the softness of her hair in his hands and thought about holding her close as he rained kisses up and down her neck.

In his mind, she wrapped her legs around his hips and her breasts pushed against his chest. His hands came to her hips and held her tight against his desire until suddenly they were skin to skin.

Her legs were still wrapped around his hips, and he was buried deep inside her and she was moaning with delight and just when he was on the verge of coming, her moans turned to screams.

He woke with a shock and was on his knees quickly with his knife in his hands.

The cave was still dark, but he could just make out her form on the ground next to him.

She was thrashing around and moaning with the nightmare. Covering his knife, he sat back down and pulled her up halfway onto his lap.

Then he gently rocked her as she woke from the nightmare.

"Shhh, you're safe." He put his hands into her hair and pulled her face to his, kissing her temple.

He felt the second she was fully awake. She tensed, and then when she realized where she was and who she was with, she relaxed and wrapped her arms around his waist.

The rain had stopped, and he could already hear life in the jungle coming awake. He knew sunrise was coming soon and they probably should get up and start the day early.

He sat there holding her, kissing her hair and forehead.

"I dreamed you left me here to run off with two dancers, then men came after me and…"

"Shhh, it won't happen," he said against her skin. "I'm not going anywhere.

Although, what did the dancers look like?"

She chuckled into his chest, a sound he was happy to hear. Then she pulled back and looked at him through the dark. He could just make out her face. He leaned down and put his lips to hers in a gentle kiss meant to soothe her.

Instead, it lit fires deep within him and made him aware of how uncomfortable it was to have her leaning across his crotch. He realized how much he wanted to pull her down on top of him so he could take her slowly as the sun rose.

"Mmm, David?" She pulled back a little, looking at him.

"Alice, we'd better get ready."

He felt her panting out of breath and smiled. "Trust me, there is nothing more that I want to be doing than making love to you now. Now is not the time or place.

Besides, I'm starved, and we could both use a shower."

She pulled back and he saw mortification cross her face as she realized they both stank of day-old sweat. He wanted to laugh. She smelled wonderful; he had been more concerned about himself.

She moved from his lap, and he instantly missed the feel of her body next to his. Standing, he tried to work out the kinks from sleeping in the same position on the hard ground.

The cave was getting lighter, which told him the sun was rising. In the dim light, he watched her shake her blanket out and start to roll it up. He walked to the mouth of the cave and decided a quick shower would be worth the chill he'd feel.

Taking the small path of rocks, he climbed down to the base of the waterfall and removed his clothes. He shook them free of dust and hung them on a low branch. He walked into the shallow end until he was in waist deep, then dove into the crystal-clear water, enjoying the freezing water as it woke his body very quickly.

A few minutes later he stood under the waterfall, allowing the water to rinse away the dirt and sweat. He was shocked to look up and see a very naked Alice jumping into the pool in front of him.

He would have laughed, but his mouth had gone dry. She was exquisite. Her long legs and arms pushed her through the water quickly as she moved to climb the stones towards the fall. He watched her as she came to stand right in front of him.

"You didn't think you were going to be the only one to enjoy such a wonderful waterfall, did you?" she yelled over the rushing water and smiled at him.

"You can shut your mouth now, David." She laughed and then closed her eyes and let the water fall over her head. He stood there and watched her, and even though the water was cold enough to have any man shivering, he felt himself getting hot.

She ran her hands over her hair and down her neck towards her breast, and he licked his lips seeing her nipples pucker in the icy water. She moved her hands over her chest and down her tight stomach, and he closed his eyes when she stopped just above the dark patch of curly hair covering her sex. How could she do this to him? Did she not get that they were totally exposed here?

He opened his eyes and saw that she was watching him with hunger in her eyes. He watched as she ran her eyes over him slowly, feeling her stare burn into him everywhere she looked. His arms, down his chest towards his light happy trial of hair that traveled to his very large, very erect sex. When she saw him, she licked her lips and he lost control.

He pushed her against the rock face just to the side of the rushing water, and then his mouth was on hers as her legs wrapped around his hips. He pushed her legs farther around his hips, lifting her higher so their sexes touched, and before she could say anything, he was imbedded deep into her heat.

Her head rolled back, and he watched her eyes go from fiery to cloudy as she moaned his name. He dipped his head and licked her exposed neck, tasting the fresh water and the sweet taste of her heated skin. He drove her deeper and harder, pushing her faster, building them both up.

Her back was pressed against the rock, and he used one hand to brace them against the nature-built wall, holding them steady as he pleased her. Her hips moved, her hands gripped his wet shoulders, and when he dipped his head to take her nipple into his mouth, she screamed his name.

He pushed her faster and harder and felt himself ready to explode as he gripped her soft butt in his hands. He leaned his forehead against the cool stone and cried out her name as she arched and tensed with her release.

Alice felt the cold stone on her back and Ethan's breath on her neck. She wouldn't regret this move. She'd always taken what she'd wanted and she'd wanted him. Especially after walking out of the cave and seeing him standing naked under the water.

She would have had to be a saint not to want to jump him. His muscles were impressive in clothes, but bare, she just wanted to lick him up and down.

As she felt his breathing slow, she knew he was going to be pissed at her for maneuvering him so easily. She'd never seduced someone like that before and she felt liberated in doing so.

She wanted to do it again, but doubted they had the time or could spare the energy. Her hands felt a few small scars on his back that she'd seen the other night when she'd been following him.

Reaching down, she ran her hand over the larger one along the lower part of his spine.

"How did you get this?" she asked as he held himself still.

"Hmm. I should have been looking behind me instead of in front."

She didn't like that he was unclear, but supposed it was a tender subject taking in account what all his past jobs must have included.

She closed her eyes for another second and enjoyed the feeling of being alive. She supposed all this had to do with what had happened yesterday. Seeing death so close, she had wanted to verify her own life, and sex had been just the tool.

"Damn!" He pulled back and frowned down at her as she unwrapped her legs from his hips. She chuckled. "I've never really gotten that kind of reaction after hot sex before."

"Uh?" He looked at her. "No, it's not... It's just that I went so fast, we didn't use protection."

She laughed harder. "It's okay, big boy. I'm clean and on the patch." She rubbed the patch on her stomach and noticed the relief flood his face.

"I'm clean, too. I was more concerned about the protection against pregnancy part."

"Don't you want kids?" she asked as she walked back under the freezing water and began rinsing herself again.

"What?" He looked up from her hands as they ran over her breast and she smiled. He was so easy. "Oh, yeah, of course. But not until later. I'm not even thirty yet."

"Oh?"

He smiled slowly as he quickly walked towards her and pulled her with him as he jumped back into the deep, cold water of the pool.

When they surfaced again, he was still smiling. He dipped his head for a fast kiss. "We need to be moving. The sun's already up. We need to travel twice as far as we did yesterday."

She tried not to, but she groaned when she heard this.

"I know, I know, but think of it this way; from here on out, it's all downhill."

Less than an hour later, she wanted to kill him again. Her thighs were screaming at her and her hands had cuts and scrapes from all the branches she'd grabbed hold of as they made their way down the very steep incline.

He hadn't been joking; it had been all downhill since they'd left the cave and the waterfall.

Oh, how she missed the cool water. The sun was barely up, and she was, once again, drenched in sweat.

She'd tied her long hair up in a braid and was thankful she'd found a small rubber band in the bottom of her bag to tie it back with.

David looked like he could use another shower. She could see sweat rolling down his back. His shirt was soaking wet between his shoulder blades.

She'd lost her footing several times, and he'd been there to grab her and hold her steady.

She knew she was taking a big chance to be with him. After all, what did she really know about David? Apparently, the arrogance had all been a show.

She knew what she'd heard from her father and her brother. Blake had called him GI Joe and he had told her in detail how he'd rushed in and rescued him from the bad men.

Her father had mentioned his long-standing record with the military and said he was the best man for the job to save Blake.

Her father had hired David's crew to watch Blake for a few months after the incident. Her father told her that he'd only met David once, on the day he had delivered Blake to him in Austin.

Since then, it had been other members of his team that had done private security when he needed them. Her father had been even more impressed that David had come along on the short journey from Dallas back to Austin with the eight-year-old, rather than trust law officials to deliver him safe and sound.

Her mind turned and she wondered if he'd slept with any of the girls that had hung in his arms.

After witnessing the power of what had happened back at the waterfall, she got the impression that it had been a while for him. For herself it had been well over six months since she'd broken things off with Scott, whom she'd dated for three months. Knowing how much she'd wanted him and how sexually shut up she'd been, she estimated by his reaction that it had been about that long since he'd enjoyed himself as well.

At least this all made perfectly good sense to her as she trudged through the jungle at a high rate of speed.

"So," she said when the ground leveled, and she felt like she could breathe again, "tell me a little about yourself. Where are you from?"

He looked over at her, and she could have sworn she saw humor in his eyes.

"So now you get to the personal questions. Don't you have it a little backwards, Princess?"

She smiled. "I guess I do. Usually, I like to meet a man's parents before I take them to a waterfall and let them…"

"Okay, okay, I get it," he interrupted her and chuckled. "I'm from a small town in Washington state. Both my parents are alive and well and I'm sure would be tickled to meet you. I have a half-sister." He broke off as he chopped a large vine that had been blocking their path with his machete. "…who was stolen as a baby.

She found us almost four years ago. She's married and living in New York with a two-year-old daughter, Rose, who is the greatest love of my life." He motioned for her to follow him down another steep incline and he stopped talking while he helped her. When she had jumped the short distance to the ground, he continued.

"I went into the Special Forces right out of high school. They came searching for me. I guess I'd placed high in the college exams." He tapped his head. "I have a wonderful memory, and they were looking for people like me.

When they got a look at me, they put me through all sorts of special training, and I guess I just fell into my job. I worked in special ops for a while until I felt it was time to retire, then I went into business for myself. Nothing more to tell. Kind of boring if you ask me." He smiled back at her.

"Boring? You call what you do boring?" She shook her head. "My father told me a little about you after you brought Blake back to us, and I wouldn't describe your life as boring."

He shrugged his shoulders and kept walking. "So, tell me about yourself."

"Oh please, you can't fool me.

You probably knew all about me before you even met me. You probably knew what color underwear I was wearing the day we met." She smiled as he stopped and turned around to face her. His forehead was creased, and he looked like he was thinking about something.

"That doesn't mean I wouldn't like to hear it from you. Hearing the personal details are far better than studying someone on paper."

He started to turn around but looked back over his shoulder. "And they were hot pink." He smiled and started walking again.

She thought about it and figured he was probably right. "Okay, what do you want to know? I assume you know where I went to college, where I got my first job, and who I have dated over the course of my entire life."

He chuckled. "Tell me why you chose journalism."

She thought about it for a minute. "When I was a girl, I used to watch the evening news with my father.

Since he was always such a busy man, it was really the only time we had to spend together. I always loved the anchor woman's hair and outfits and could picture myself dressed up, telling the interesting stories I was hearing. I dressed up as an anchorwoman for Halloween every year until I was thirteen." He chuckled.

"I can totally see that," he said causing her to smile.

"It was one of the only careers my father ever truly gave his full blessing for. My other career choices weren't so notable."

He stopped and looked at her. "Really? What other choices did you have in mind?"

"She smiled and walked past him. "Well, in high school I decided I wanted to be a flight attendant or a stripper." He pulled her arm until she stopped and looked at him.

"Well, I'd spent the night at a friend's house, and we'd watched Flash dance. The movie made it look so glamorous; I'd rushed home to my father and told him that I had found what I wanted to do with my life.

"She chuckled.

"He banned me from ever seeing that friend again.

He smiled and pushed aside a strand of her hair that had been pulled from her braid.

"Well, if you ever want to change careers, you can always try your routines out on me first." She punched his shoulder playfully.

Then she walked ahead of him into a clearing and stopped dead in her tracks.

There, in the middle of the jungle, stood five large men with machine guns.

Chapter 8

The Bumping Ride

David pulled her back into the brush quickly and didn't wait to see if they'd been spotted as they took off running back the way they'd come. When they'd made it twenty yards he chanced a glance over his shoulder and saw several heads bobbing in the trees, heading their way. Damn!

He grabbed her arm, and they made a sharp turn, cutting to the right down a path he knew was dangerous. He didn't think they had any choice. He didn't know if the men where the one's looking for them. Hell, they could have stumbled on a drug deal or something else.

All he knew was they couldn't chance stopping and asking them what they wanted.

"Sorry, Princess. It's going to be a bumpy ride. He grabbed her and flung himself off the cliff, trying to take the brunt of the impact himself.

The rains the night before helped their muddy journey down the slippery ravine.

As they slid down the steep hill, David mumbled every time his back connected with a sharp stick or rock. Alice howled and held onto his shoulders.

"Quiet!" He tried to get her to stop screaming. If they played their cards right, the men would just assume they'd been lost in the forest and wouldn't think they were dumb enough to slide down a two-hundred-foot cliff on their backs.

60

Finally, he could feel his force slowing and felt a little relieved. He chanced a look ahead of them and almost screamed at himself. There in front of him was a great drop off. He let go of Alice with one hand and reached for anything to stop their speed.

Damn! They were heading for the edge, and he had no clue what was at the bottom. "Grab hold of something," he groaned. She began to frantically grab hold of tiny twigs and branches as they flew by their heads.

Finally, about ten feet from the edge, he grabbed hold of a large vine and felt himself slowing. When the vine ripped out of the ground from their weight, he dug his hand into the ground as Alice held onto his waist. Mud coated his back and legs and he even felt some down his pants.

Finally, they came to a slow stop less than two feet from the rocky edge.

They lay there, holding each other, breathing heavily. He rested his head back in the mud and looked up through the thick leaves to the blue sky above, thanking God, they had stopped.

He heard shouting and pushed himself up, pulling her with him. He rushed to the edge and looked over and was happy to see a deep river about twenty feet below them.

"We aren't done with the ride yet, Princess. Make sure to cross your feet when you land." He grabbed her hand and when she nodded, they both jumped as far as they could into the open air.

He'd ridden plenty of water slides as a kid, and he'd had his share of solo jumps out of airplanes, but nothing prepared him for the drop into the unknown, especially since Alice's hand was still in his.

They must have hit the water at thirty miles per hour. The wind was knocked from his lungs and Alice's hand was ripped from his.

He fought to control his extremities and then realized that his heavy backpack was weighing him down.

Using his legs, he easily broke through the surface of the water and looked around for Alice. When he couldn't find her, he thought about her heavy backpack.

Escaping under the rushing water, he searched for her. The unstable water was muddy, and he could barely make out his own hand in front of his face. Removing his heavy bag, he kicked under the surface again and this time felt around with his hands and feet.

When he kicked something with his boot, he reached down and grabbed a handful of hair and quickly pulled her up. She grabbed his hand, and he rushed them to the top.

When they broke the surface, Alice began to spit up water and cough. They were being pushed down river by the quickly flowing water. He put his arm under her shoulders and kicked towards the left embankment.

They were picking up too much speed and the river had widened, and when he tried kicking again, it felt like the shore was getting farther away.

"David?" Alice noticed that the water was getting faster, no doubt from all the rain last night.

"I know, I know. Help me kick towards shore. Come on." They started kicking together and had made it almost to the shore when he heard the loud sounds of more rushing water.

He looked over and saw the spray of a large waterfall that they were heading right towards.

"Kick, Alice!" He used all his leg muscles and thought he felt the bottom of the river. It took a few more kicks before he could dig his toes into the pebbles and dirt at the river's bottom.

The rushing water started carrying Alice out of his arms, but he grabbed onto her bag and held on as she gripped the shoulder straps.

Her head went under the water several times as he forced his body against the flow of the water. He was totally focused on each step, but suddenly noticed that her weight had disappeared. He freaked out, thinking she'd fallen out of the arm holds of her backpack. He looked back and saw her moving beside him, taking each step he took, trying to make it to shore.

She smiled over at him, and he knew he had lost a part of his heart.

How could this have happened so quickly? A woman would smile as if she was looking at the gates of heaven after what they'd just been through deserved better than him.

He was a soldier, a drone, used to doing other people's hard and dirty work. He didn't deserve someone who took sunshine with her everywhere she went.

When they collapsed on the muddy shore, he looked around for his bag, hoping that it had somehow come ashore. He tried to measure how far they'd gone and looked back upriver to see if the men were still chasing them.

He estimated that they'd traveled a few miles. He didn't notice anyone following them, but that could change. They needed to get away from the water and quickly.

He looked over at Alice. She was resting the back of her head on the grassy shore. Mud was caked into her hair and her clothes were soaked and muddy. Her eyes were closed as she leveled her breathing.

"We must get moving, Princess. The men might be right behind us."

She nodded and started to rise, her bag still on her shoulders. He reached over and took it from her.

"Since I lost mine, I'll carry the extra weight." She smiled and nodded again. He wondered why she wasn't talking and asked, "Is your throat okay?"

She coughed a few times, then whispered. "I think I drank too much water and dirt. It will be fine, after I get a drink."

He stopped and allowed her to pull out her canteen of water. As she took a drink, he realized most of the food had been in his bag. He could have kicked himself for not looking ahead and being smart enough to put some more in hers.

He'd never lost his bag before. Never. He'd just have to deal with that later.

Right now, they needed to get as far away from the water as they could.

"Here, walk on the dry spots so we don't leave tracks." He held out his hand and showed her where to step. She followed his instructions and then he said, "Go stand under that tree."

She walked over and after checking the branches for snakes, leaned against the trunk. He broke off a small branch and tried to wipe away their exit from the river. It wasn't perfect, but it would have to do. He threw the branch into the bushes and met her under the tree. Grabbing her hand, they started walking quickly.

"How do you know where we are? If we are even heading in the right direction?"

He tapped his head.

"Oh, come on. You can't have a map in that big head of yours."

He chuckled at her. He jumped a small ravine and then turned to help her across.

"I have a photographic memory. My sister has it, too. I guess we got it from our mom. I could never get away with anything when I lived at home." He chuckled again.

She watched his back, almost tripping over a small tree that had fallen.

"Well? Go on…"

He turned and looked over his shoulder at her.

"What?"

"Tell me about your mother."

He smiled and held a large branch aside for her. She noticed he made a point not to break it. If anyone was following them, they would have a hard path to follow.

She felt like they were zigzagging through the jungle, turning at every third tree. She noticed they never headed in the same direction for too long. If he did have a map in that brain of his, she was very impressed.

"Well, I was raised as an only child, so I got too much attention from my loving parents.

At times I wished for my older sister's return so I could have someone to take the blame once and a while. No matter what I did or said, my mother's memory was long and always correct."

"How about your dad?"

"My dad is a lot like me. He likes to hunt, fish, and spend time with his two brothers. They live near my parents in Washington. My parents had known each other all their lives, but a year after my sister was stolen, they fell in love and married. I came along a while later."

"I always wanted a sister or brother, too. I guess that's why I was so happy when Blake came along. Even though he's half my age, I spoil him." She smiled and realized that they had more in common than she'd thought they did to begin with.

An hour before nightfall, Alice was so worn out she could barely lift her feet.

Her clothes were wrinkled and dirty, her hair had come undone from the braid, and she just felt weary.

She could see that David didn't look any better than she felt. Not having to carry her bag did help a lot, but her feet were just so heavy, she desperately wanted to stop for the night.

"David?" He stopped and turned to look at her. "Can we stop soon?" She could see him think about it, then he looked around like he was trying to judge where they were.

There was no possibility that he knew where they were. They had continued to zigzag through the thick forest for the remainder of the day.

At this point, she wasn't even sure which way the sun was setting. The clouds were thick and hung low in the trees. There was even a mist hanging around the top of the trees. It was still in the high eighties, and she wanted another shower in a cold waterfall.

"There's a small creek with a pool near here. It's only about half a mile away. Can you make it that far so we can clean up?" She nodded.

Okay, so if he knew there was a creek a half a mile away, she was going to stop underestimating him.

A short while later, they cautiously approached the stream. There was a very small waterfall and the water was only a few feet deep, just deep enough that she could probably sit in it. There was no cave in case it rained again that night.

They'd just have to get wet. She'd gauged all this as he was scouting out the area to make sure no one was around.

"It's a popular camping site," he told her as they sat by the stream. "We're about half a day's hike from civilization. There are a few small towns we will must pass through. We'd better do it in the middle of the night, so we aren't seen by anyone."

She nodded her head in agreement, but in truth she was only half listening to him. She'd sat down by the pool on a large round rock and had removed her shoes.

Nasty red blisters covered her heels and when she dipped her feet into the cool water, she almost cried at the relief it provided. She stood up and walked cautiously over the large rocks right into the clear water, clothes, and all.

She turned and watched him set the bag down and do the same. He smiled at her.

"You know, you sure are taking all this very well." He stopped right in front of her and sat down.

"How else would I take all this?" She ducked down and leaned back to rinse the dirt and sweat from her hair. Using her hands, she tried to wash the dirt from her clothes. She'd almost forgotten she'd dyed her hair black until she loosened her braid and the dark stresses surrounded her face.

"Well, I thought you'd be doing a lot of crying and complaining," he said sitting next to her, trying to scrub himself clean. The rocky bottom of the small pool was a little hard to get comfortable on, but she finally found a flat rock and propped herself on it."

She laughed. "Normally I would have." She raised her legs up and looked at her bare feet. His boots were still on, and she knew that it would take a few hours for them to dry. "But since it's all my fault that we're in this mess, I thought I'd leave the complaining to a minimum."

"Alice"

"No, don't. We've been over this. I don't know what I'd do without you, David." She tried to hold back the emotions.

He pulled her close and they started floating in the water together.

"You know, if you imagine hard enough, I bet you could convince your mind we're in some fancy hotel in Ponce, sipping margaritas and having the time of our lives."

She closed her eyes and allowed her mind to float away. She woke a few hours later to David pulling on her arm. He must have carried her out of the water after she'd fallen asleep floating with him.

"Alice," he whispered, "we must go. Put on your boots." She blinked a few times and then she could hear it. Quickly sitting up, she realized they were laying in the grass near the water's edge. Her boots were within arm's reach.

She threw them on and was ready to run when she recognized several words being spoken by the approaching people.

"David," she whispered to him, "they're American."

"It doesn't matter. Come on." He pulled her arm, and they started moving quietly in the opposite direction.

The voices continued as if they hadn't heard them. Soon they were so far away, they couldn't hear anything except night noises.

She didn't want to be walking anymore. The only plus was that the moon was full. She could see clearly enough to follow him, but she could have used a few more hours of sleep. They walked for what seemed an hour before he finally stopped.

"We can spend the rest of the night here. There's a nice sandy riverbed where we can camp. He sat and pulled her bag into his lap and started searching the large section in the dark.

Finally, he pulled out one of the bags of food she'd placed in her bag and handed it to her. They ate in silence and then he pulled her down into his arms. She fell back asleep leaning against him in the soft sand with the large moon overhead.

He watched the stars and the clouds as they crossed in front of the moon, blocking out its rays. His mind just wouldn't shut down. Thoughts of her consumed him.

He'd never had this hard of a time clearing his mind before. She was just a job. He'd had plenty of jobs that he'd wanted to get close to. Plenty of women that would have been easy to enjoy. He'd kept his private life separate and it had worked out well so far.

Then he remembered the waterfall and his mind played over the scene of Alice diving into the water naked. He thought of her swimming, her long legs and arms moving towards him. He saw her pulling her wet body from the water and walking slowly towards him. No, she wasn't just a job. He pulled her closer and closed his eyes.

Chapter 9

In Panic

David woke to the sun in his eyes and was shocked. He'd never slept so deeply. Then he realized he was alone, and panic overtook him. Sitting up quickly, he nudged when he heard Alice say from behind him.

"I'm over here. Don't worry, I didn't go far. Just had to clean up." She dropped her bag next to him and smiled. "You look like you could use a couple more hours of sleep."

He'd been having a nightmare about a job he'd done a few years back. He'd woken still able to hear the men chasing him, and the client, an old friend, screaming his name as he slowly died. It had been almost seven years ago, but it still felt like yesterday.

His back ached where the long scar covered his spine; he'd barely made it out of Afghanistan alive. Having another close friend literally stab you in the back made you reevaluate your friends.

Ivan had been there for him. He's the one that had nursed him back to health until he was well enough to fly home. He'd thought about retiring then but had stuck it out a few more years.

He'd been sick then and had slept for a week. Now he felt like he could sleep at least that long, which was totally throwing him off. His head hurt, his back hurt, his feet hurt. Hell, everything hurt. He frowned and tried to assess why he wasn't feeling so hot. He quickly tore off his clothes and started checking himself.

"Not that I'm going to complain about you getting naked, but what's with the strip show?"

"Help me check for small bites." He motioned to his back. "They'll be two small red spots, maybe with a white circle around it."

She started running her hands over his shoulders slowly. "Nothing," she said and he stood up and dropped his pants quickly. She gasped and said, "Here." She circled a small section on his upper thigh.

"But it's red and swollen, not white."

He relaxed a little. "Okay, whew. That was a close one." He started to pull up his pants.

"What? What does that mean? Shouldn't you put something on it? Do I need to suck out the poison?" She tried to keep him from pulling his pants back up.

"No," he chuckled, "it's just a small snake bite." He pulled the pants up.

"What would it have been if it was white?"

"Spider bite," he said and zipped his pants.

"So, snakes are better than spiders?"

He frowned. "No, not normally."

She crossed her arms and looked at him, obviously waiting for more information.

"I was bitten by a snake a few years back. Same kind of thing, I felt aching for a day or two then was back to normal.

Most likely it's the same thing this time. Once I was bit by a poisonous spider, and I spent almost a month in the hospital. Almost lost my foot."

She gasped, and he could see her blushing, trying to make herself smaller and looking around.

"Don't worry, Princess. It's very rare to get bitten. I just happened to sit on a nest while I was on lookout a few years back. The guys in my group never let me hear the end of it, though."

He bent to pick up his shirt and shook it out, then put it back on. He thought he heard her sigh when he was fully covered again.

"Let's see what else you've got in this bag to eat."

He sat next to the bag on the soft sand and started searching through the items she'd grabbed from Ivan's shelves.

"This will come in handy." He pulled out a small medical box and opened it.

Then he popped two aspirins into his mouth and swallowed quickly. Hopefully they'd take care of the aches. Then his hand hit another box and when he pulled out the silver case, he was shocked and happy. He'd lost his weapon when his bag sank to the bottom of the river.

"Wow, I'm impressed, Princess." He smiled at her as she sat next to him.

He opened the small case and smiled at the .45 and was even happier when he noticed a box of bullets sitting beside it in the waterproof case.

She reached past him and dug into the bag and pulled out a sealed bag of energy bars. Handing him one, she ripped one open and bit into it. Her eyes closed and she moaned.

How could he go from protection mode to horny in under five seconds flat?

Damn, she was doing something to him. Even though they both looked a mess, having worn the same clothes for two days now, and her hair was in knots and she has some mud on her cheek, she still looked beautiful.

He lifted his hand and wiped the dry dirt from her face. She stopped and looked at him with questioning eyes.

"I'm sorry you must go through all this. You were made to sleep in fancy hotels, not on the hard ground. For eating at the best restaurants, not eating energy bars like this," he said, waving the energy bar."

"Why do you say stuff like that? Did you know that some of my fondest memories as a child are of camping with my dad?" She pouted a little which only made him look at her lips, making him realize how kissable they were.

He smiled and ate his energy bar.

"You think I'm joking, or you just don't believe me." She frowned even more. "Have you heard one complaint from me since we started this journey?"

He thought about it and couldn't remember her saying anything other than asking to stop for the night. He knew she wasn't used to hiking round the clock like he was.

He did what he had to get the job done. If it meant having a few sleepless nights, then he'd catch up on his sleep later. She hadn't complained once. He smiled at her. She really was a lot tougher than she looked.

"We'd better get moving. Tonight, we'll make it through the outskirts of town. Hopefully by this time tomorrow we'll be on a plane to New York."

"Why New York?" She took a deep drink of her water and he noticed that they were low on fluids.

"I've got connections in that city. We can book safe passage to other States without raising any flags."

He stood and dusted off his pants, then reached to help her up. Just for his pleasure, he pulled her into his arms and kissed her until he felt her body melting against his.

They walked for a few hours, and he made sure they weren't being followed, constantly looking over his shoulder and listening for anyone else around.

So far all he could hear were the sounds of the jungle. They'd just walked into a small clearing when Alice gasped, and he went on guard. He was ready to grab her and run when she started laughing.

"Oh, look at them, there are so many!" Her face was turned to the sky and when he looked up, he saw hundreds of birds. The green, yellow, and blue colored parrots hopped from limb to limb.

He could hear their calls as they flew around enjoying the nuts and berries from the trees high above.

He watched Alice's face light up and couldn't help but smile as she watched the display.

"They are so beautiful. I can't believe how many there are."

He enjoyed seeing the birds, but he enjoyed watching her enjoyment even more. Her whole face lit up. Her smile was contagious and by the time they started walking again, he had forgotten about the aches and pains from the snake bite.

They walked for another hour and then stopped at a stream to eat a lunch consisting of another power bar each. They rested for a while, enjoying the quiet of their surroundings.

"We have about two more hours before we're going to have to stop until dark, then we can sneak into town."

"How are we going to fly to New York? If there are lookouts all over, won't we be spotted at the airports?"

He smiled. "Not this airport. Trust me, they won't be looking for us where we're going."

They made it to the edge of town without any problems. He made a makeshift lookout in one of the trees and helped Ann climb up so they would be hidden if anyone should pass by.

Just after midnight, they climbed down and quickly made their way down the sidewalks past all the small, closed shops.

The crumbled storefronts were gated and chained up for the night. The streets were made of dirt and full of large holes that would have wrecked even the largest truck tires. They didn't see another soul the entire two dozen blocks they walked.

Passing the stores, they made it to the outskirts of all the small huts where he knew they might run into problems. They had it easy so far, since all the shops were closed. Here, where the small brick and clay buildings had been erected as if thrown together by a roll of the dice, the streets were littered with men.

"Stay close," he whispered as he pulled her closer.

He knew they had another dozen blocks to go through the huts before they'd reach the outskirts of San Juan International Airport. They'd made it almost eight blocks before two men started following them.

He doubted they were specifically looking for them, just trouble. Maybe they'd try to steal his bag, maybe they just wanted a fight, or maybe they wanted something worse. He pulled Alice closer.

"Sorry, looks like tonight is going to be a little exciting after all. Don't run when it starts. Stay close no matter what."

She nodded and he could feel the tension in her body next to his.

Less than a block later, the men made their move, and it was exactly what he'd counted on.

They'd had another buddy run ahead and come out in front of them with a knife. When the skinny man jumped out from the corner, his two buddies quickly came up behind and tried to grab Alice's arm.

David was shocked when he saw Alice dip and turn. She kicked out and hit the man, square in his chest, knocking him to the ground. He gasped for breath, holding his chest, while rolling around in the dirt.

It took David a few seconds to recover, but he blocked the skinny man's attempt to stab him by breaking his nose with his fist. The man dropped the knife and grabbed his face, then took off running in the opposite direction from were they'd just come.

The third man was a lot bigger, more David's size, and when he tried to reach for Alice, she dropped to the ground and rolled away from him like a stealthy ninja.

The man didn't see David coming. It took two blows to the side of his head to have him lying in a heap on the dirt road.

The conscious man on the ground was still gasping for breath as David walked over and picked him up by the front of his shirt.

"It hurts, doesn't it?" he asked the man. David held him still by holding the front of his shirt in his fist. "Breathe, take deep breaths."

74

He smiled over at Alice as she crossed her arms and looked like she was trying to decide if he was crazy.

"What? I need to ask him some questions. If he can't breathe, how is he supposed to answer me?"

He looked back at the man and saw that his coloring was coming back. "The woman can kick, huh?" he asked his attacker.

When the man just nodded, he continued. "What were you trying to do? Steal from us?" The man nodded again. "Did anyone send you?"

The man looked up at him like he was crazy, then shook his head no. "Good, okay. You can go." He pushed the man down the street. He stopped, then looked at his friend and back at David.

"You can have him, we're done." David grabbed Alice's hand and started walking again.

When they reached the chain link fence around the airport a few blocks later, they walked around to the guard tower, and he saw his good buddy sitting where he knew he'd be.

Frank was easily three hundred pounds. His body mass ate up most of the small booth. David walked up to him and gave him a big hug as he greeted him.

"Frank, this is Alice. Alice, Frank." He pulled Alice to his side and smiled at Frank.

His friends eyes lit up and he could see the situation register in his face.

"Nice to meet you, Alice." He smiled at David.

"What are you doing back here? I thought after the last time, Ivan told you to stay out of Ponce."

David laughed. "We made up. I need transport to New York, and it has to be on the down low."

David held his hand flat and motioned below his knees. Frank whistled. "I don't know, man. There hasn't been anything like that come through in weeks. I do have something.

You may not like the accommodations, though."

"We'll take it."

Frank looked at Alice, then back at him. "Are you sure? Your girl here might not like that she can't sit in first class."

David smiled. He liked that Frank had called Alice his girl. "My girl here can handle whatever you throw at her."

"I 'thought we had them in the jungle, but they disappeared down the river. Jumped from a hundred-foot cliff." The phone call was cutting in and out and he could barely make out all the words. "You were right to have us checking the trails.

We'll keep watch. The last we saw them; they were heading north. We'll have them, there aren't too many places they can hide. Plus, they were traveling light.

There is no way they had enough supplies to last too long in the jungle."

He didn't even look up when someone walked into the room.

"Just take care of it, I'm tired of this thing scary over my head. I'll expect you to deal with this."

He hung up the phone and looked at his employer.

"Have you got my speech finalized yet?"

"Yes, sir. I'll print it out for you right now and bring it in to you."

He stood and walked down the hall to the copy room, loathing, and hatred in his heart. His boss deserved everything that was coming to him. If they didn't find the girl, then he'd have to come up with another plan. It wasn't as if he wasn't good at thinking on his feet, it's just that he knew the right buttons to push and he'd picked the best possible method to obtain his and his boss's goals.

Chapter 10

The Cargo Plane

Alice sat uncomfortably in the large wooden crate. The open slats allowed for the cold air flowing through from the cargo hold of the airplane. David sat across from her like he was comfortable.

"How long do we have to sit in this box?" she yelled over the loud noises of the engines.

"The whole trip to New York. Come over here." He motioned to the side he was sitting on and smiled.

She couldn't refuse him. That smile did something to her insides. He put his arm around her and she snuggled into his chest. He was so warm she immediately realized how cold she was and started shivering.

"Aren't we going to suffocate or something? I know in regular airplanes they must keep pumping air into the cabins."

He chuckled at her.

"That's why we're on this small cargo plane instead of a bigger one. It won't reach that high of an altitude. The downside of it is it will take us twice as long to get where we are going."

He started rubbing his hand over her hair and she realized how wonderfully normal it felt, how right she felt in his arms. Looking up at him, she realized he'd been watching her, and when she looked at him, he pulled her up and kissed her lightly. His mouth caused sparks all the way down to her toes.

There wasn't a lot of room in the crate they were in, only enough that they'd laid out a sleeping bag to sit on. His legs could stretch across without being bent and she could have easily curled up and fallen asleep comfortably.

When the kiss deepened, she rose above him, straddling him as he took her hips in his hands.

She'd been burning for him since the waterfall. It was hard to explain, but she'd felt hollow since that encounter. She'd never experienced anything quite like the feeling of David inside her.

In every relationship in the past, she'd always been the one in control. She'd prided herself on that. She'd never really needed or wanted someone as badly as she wanted him right now.

Even with the circumstances being what they were, she wanted him. Taking her time, she inched her hands down his chest and slowly removed his shirt. When his hands hit the top of the box, they both chuckled.

"Alice, what are we doing? He asked when his shirt was off. I am sorry, sir, they seem to have slipped through my hands. She smiled. "I would think that was rather obvious."

He smiled in return, "You know what I mean," he said as she trailed kisses down his neck.

"We have hours and hours we're going to be stuck in this box. We're just going to enjoy ourselves and take our minds off the fact that it's cold and uncomfortable in here."

When he smiled and started to pull her shirt off, she knew he agreed with her plan. They worked out a system for removing each other's clothes and soon they were skin to skin as she connected his hips again.

His hands were running over her back as he pulled her closer to kiss every inch of her face and neck. When she tried to trail kisses down his chest, her feet hit the other side of the box and she had to bend herself so she could continue her downward path, exploring and enjoying every inch of his tan muscular body.

"Alice, you're killing me," he moaned when she flicked her tongue over his flat nipple. Then she had him moaning when she lightly ran her fingernails over his skin and trailed kisses after them.

His hands balled into fists, and she could tell he was trying not to take over. She wanted control now and she was going to drive him mad.

Her fingers traveled down the light trail of hair that went to his sex and she enjoyed seeing him shy away when she ran a finger over him.

Next, she ran her mouth down the same path and his hands fisted in her hair when her tongue touched him.

She was good at this. She'd prided herself on the fact that she'd always enjoyed giving pleasure as much as she enjoyed getting it.

When she moved to take him completely in her mouth, he pulled her up and growled at her.

"You little devil." He smiled as he pulled her down, so she was under him.

As he hovered over her, he said, "I know what you're doing." He chuckled. "Not this time, Princess."

Then he was kissing the same path on her, and she forgot her plan of controlling the situation. For the first time, she enjoyed the feeling of losing herself in the moment.

He ran his hands and his mouth down her heated skin, leaving a trail that tingled. She felt like putty under his hands as they molded her curves, and when he ran a finger gently over her, she arched up, seeking more contact. He chuckled and she realized what he was doing. He'd taken complete control of her, and she hadn't minded.

The smirk on his face told her that he knew it, but the heat in his eyes told her he wasn't unaffected. He was moving slowly, running his hands over her, circling when she wanted him to touch her again.

She tried to move and get him to speed things up, but he just smiled down at her and said, "We have all the time in the world. I just want to enjoy you, Princess."

She groaned, not knowing how much more she could stand his torture.

"David, you're killing me."

Finally, he touched her where she wanted, and she almost came undone in his hands. How did it come to this? She'd wanted to show him pleasure. Now as she felt herself building up, she watched his eyes and realized she was. The look on his face told her everything.

Reaching up, she grabbed his hair and pulled him back down to her mouth.

When he was an inch away, he paused, and she could have sworn she saw more than just desire cross his eyes.

As they kissed, she realized this position was not going to work. He was on his hands and knees and there just wasn't enough room in the crate to continue with her lying down.

Rolling over herself, she took his shoulders and pushed him down until he was lying with his feet flat on the bottom and his knees slightly bent. Then she connected him again, bending down so her head wouldn't hit the top of the box.

"This isn't as easy as I'd hoped." She smiled down at him. He pulled her hips towards him and she leaned down to kiss him deeply as she slid slowly onto him.

She watched as he threw his head back and closed his eyes. His mouth was slightly open, and she watched as the muscles on his neck and arms flexed. She smiled and ran her hands over them.

His hands went to her hips and dug into her soft flesh as he moved her. She enjoyed the feeling of him and couldn't hold back much longer. When he reached for her and ran his fingers over her lightly, she felt the explosion rip from her, deep inside.

"Again," he growled as he continued to pump faster and harder, building her up again. His hand went to her nipple, tugging lightly.

Then he leaned up and used his mouth on her heated skin, building her faster and faster. He braced his legs wide on the ground and bucked under her as she rode him, her knees tucked close to his hips, her hands on his chest, enjoying the play of muscles.

Just when she thought she couldn't take it any longer, she heard him growl her name, and she threw her head back and joined him.

David lay there feeling Alice's breath on his chest and knew she was fast asleep. He listened to the loud sounds of the cargo plane and wondered what the hell, he was doing.

The number one rule in this business was, and always has been, don't get involved with a client.

So far, he'd followed that rule. There had been plenty of times he'd wanted to cross that line, but none like this. None like her. He'd felt the shock the first time he'd seen her. He'd known he should call the job off before they'd left for Ponce.

He'd even tried to keep her pissed at him by always showing off women around. It had worked for a while. He could tell she was totally turned off by him, and at one point, he was pretty sure she had called her boss to try and get him fired.

It wasn't up to Anthony if he stayed or went. Senator Rhodes was the one calling all the shots, and if he knew that he was sleeping with his daughter...

Hell, he wasn't just sleeping with her. He couldn't fool himself for much longer.

She was everything he'd ever dreamed of smart, intelligent, sexy. The fact that she could chest kick a man without breaking a sweat turned him on even more.

He felt her shiver from the cold air and pulled the sleeping bag over her. She mumbled something and snuggled deeper into his chest. He smelled rain and mud in her hair and realized it, too, was turning him on. Yup, he was a goner. He had some thinking to do. It was a good thing they'd be stuck in the crate for a few more hours.

His mind kept jumping back and forth. She was just a job, she was more than just a job. This was the first time in his adult life that he couldn't make up his mind.

It was almost as if he could feel the little angel and devil characters on his shoulders. One telling him to go for it, the other saying to step back and be good.

He'd never struggled with anything like this before. He'd never had a serious relationship before.

Sure, he'd dated. He wasn't one to deny himself the pleasure of a beautiful woman. It had been months since he'd thought about being with anyone. He supposed it was because he was just busy.

No, he couldn't fool himself. After seeing what his sister, Roberta, had with her husband, Ric, he had wanted something more than just a fling. He'd wanted what they had. What his parents and grandparents had.

Alice snuggled closer to him, and he knew without a doubt what he wanted.

He was still struggling with how to make her see that he was what she wanted, too.

A few hours later, when he felt the plane slowing and making its descent, he shook Alice awake.

"Come on, Princess, we're landing." He shook her again. She tried to snuggle back into him, so he removed the sleeping bag, so they were fully exposed.

When she felt the cold air hit her, she sat up and tried to pull the bag back. "I guess you don't mind customs seeing you naked."

That got her moving. She dressed quickly and he laughed as she struggled to put her clothes back on in the confined space. It was too close of quarters, so he had to wait until she was fully dressed to slip on his own clothes.

"Are we really going to have to go through customs? How are we going to explain…?"

"Hang on with all the questions until I get my pants on." She tried to help him slip his legs into his pants, but she only ended up making it worse.

By the time both his legs were in his pants, they were both laughing very hard and he had sweat rolling down his back.

Three hours later, they were still in the box, and he could tell she was starting to worry. They'd been moved several times, once by a large forklift, the other by two men who were speaking Spanish.

They made sure to hold still while the two men pushed the crate into the back of a large truck. They'd been driving along for almost a half hour when the truck finally came to a stop and the back was opened.

"Señor Smith, Señorita Rhodes, are you still breathing in there?"

David laughed. "Raul, get your skinny butt up here and let us out of this damn box."

"What do you mean they aren't in Ponce anymore?"

He wanted to throw the phone across the room, but it might cause too many heads to turn.

After all, it was a black-tie affair. He was standing off in a dark hallway, trying to keep his voice down.

"Where the hell are they?"

"Well, as far as we can tell they are still in the Caribbean."

"Can you narrow it down any further?" He was losing his patience.

"Not now. Is there anything you can find out on your end that might help us?"

He looked around and thought about it. "I'll get back to you." Then hung up the phone and went to join the crowd again.

Chapter 11

Guatemala

Alice wondered how many people David knew and how he knew so many in Guatemala.

She knew the kind of jobs he'd done. Most, she had assumed, were like the one he'd done for her father.

After being released from the box, she'd been shocked to discover they were in paradise. Everything was so green, it almost hurt her eyes. When she'd stood up, David had taken her arm to steady her since her legs were asleep.

"Walk a little, you'll get the feeling back in your legs." He hadn't even looked overwhelmed by spending almost twelve hours in that crate. She, on the other hand, could use a long, hot shower and a change of clothes.

When she started walking to stretch her legs, she ended up near the rim of a large cliff overlooking the ocean. She could just make out the city far off in the distance.

She'd never been to the islands before, and but this was a new experience, she was amazed at the fact that the city appeared to sit right on the edge of the cliff.

It was almost as if it were going to spill out into the water from the cliff's edge. The greenness of it all almost overwhelmed her. It was still early morning and she could see the mist and fog clinging to the tops of tall buildings.

David walked up beside her, smiling. "We have the place to ourselves for two days, then we head out.

Raul has assured me everything is to leave on Tuesday." He waved as the truck started driving away with his friend in the cab.

"What do you say to a hot shower and some new clothes? Or would you rather eat breakfast first?"

She couldn't help it, the thought of being clean and eating some real food made her jump into his arms as she squealed like a schoolgirl.

He whirled her around a few times and then set her back on her feet, smiling down at her. "Come on then, let's go get cleaned up and eat."

He walked her towards a large glass house which sat near the edge of the cliff. The blue metal roof mixed with the tall walls made the place shine. She couldn't get over the fact that she could see right through to the back of the place.

There was a large sunken living area with tan couches and bright red throw pillows. The large tile-top dining room table had chairs of the same tan and a large wooden bowl set on it.

She saw a large, frosted glass wall and thought that the bedroom and bathroom would be behind it for privacy. Through the back of the house she could see a large wooden deck and a blue tiled swimming pool with a huge fountain in the middle.

Palm trees lined the back of the pool area and surrounded the house. The house took up most of the cliff, but there was a large chunk that housed a four-car garage that had an apartment above it. Looking around, she didn't see any other homes nearby.

She stood there and admired the architecture of the place.

"Do you like it?" David asked as he stood beside her.

She didn't know what to say, so she just nodded her head. It was the most beautiful thing she'd ever seen.

"I'm glad. I had the same reaction when I bought it seven years ago."

She was shocked. She turned and looked at him. He owned this place. Why did he have a house in this island? So many other questions ran through her head.

"Shut it down for a while, Princess. Let's go get some grub and clean up, then I'll explain everything."

When she'd walked into the large bedroom, which was indeed behind the wall of frosted glass, she saw a small silver bikini. So, after hitting the shower quickly, she rushed out to the large stone tiled pool. There she floated in the cool, blue water until David came out in a pair of swim trunks and joined her.

He was carrying an ice blue fruity drink and a beer. Her drink even had a slice of pineapple on the rim of the crystal glass and had a cherry floating in it.

"I could get used to this," she said as she floated on her back with her dark hair pooling around her face.

She stopped to take a drink and moaned with delight when the sweet and tangy drink hit her mouth.

"Where did you learn to make this?" She held up her drink.

He chuckled. "I had to go undercover as a bartender in Cancun for a few months.

You wouldn't believe the tips you get there. That's how I bought this place," he said, smiling.

"Yeah, right." She chuckled at his joke. "Why here?" They were splashing side by side as she held her drink close, taking a few more sips and enjoying the icy drink.

"It seemed right. I've been here so often, buying a house here was just the natural thing to do. It was between here and Ponce and I have better connections here.

Besides, Raul is a very close friend who looks after the place. He stays in the guest house above the garage year-round. I saved his mother and sister once, so in his mind, he'll never work off the debt he thinks he owes me.

Of course, I pay him very, very well, which keeps his family happy and healthy."

She smiled at him, "Do you own any other property?"

He nodded, and she could tell he was trying to avoid answering.

"I have a condo just outside of Austin that my mother left me when she died."

She felt the alcohol in the drink relaxing her entire body. Normally one fruity drink wouldn't have affected her this much, but it had been almost twenty-four hours since she'd had anything substantial to eat.

"I've got two other places. One by my parents' place in Washington, so when I visit them, I don't bug them too much. The other is in the south of France.

What do you say to a cookout? I noticed Raul had stocked the fridge with some steaks. I've got a state-of-the-art grill and some mad skills as a chef." He smiled and she noticed how his eyes lit up.

Later, they sat around the outside patio eating grilled steak and vegetables.

They finished talking about his travels. It seemed to Alice that he'd been everywhere.

He'd also had as many fake jobs as he had different names. She giggled at some of the names and laughed at some of the jobs. Her favorite was when he'd been a male stripper in Vegas under the name of Sergeant Pecker.

"The worst part of that gig was that I had to wear these stupid police outfit, but I made really good tips." He smiled and she couldn't help falling a little more for him.

"How about the worst job?" she asked still laughing. She didn't realize the kind of hardships he might have with his jobs, until after she watched his face fall. Then she thought, really thought about what it was he did.

"David?" She reached out and took his hand.

"No, it's okay. It is part of my job, losing someone. It just hurts more when it's a kid." He took a swig of his beer. "It was almost a year before I took the job for your dad.

This little girl had been snatched from day care. Her father was a diplomat in Kenya. Well, when things got ugly a few years back... Anyway, that was the hardest I've had to deal with, seeing her... after..."

She could tell he was having a hard time with the story. He took another sip of his beer. "They let a pack of wild dogs have her." He closed his eyes and her heart broke. "She was only four and they treated her like she was meat. All because her daddy wanted change for his country."

She reached over and took his hand. "David, I'm so sorry."

"But then there are the good days." She could see he was trying to remove that image from his mind. His eyes flashed to another scene, a happier scene.

"A few years back I did this job for a friend of the family. It was one of my new brother-in-law's friends. I didn't know the connection at the time, but I can still remember this young girl's face.

She is an artist, a very talented girl. Her family was one of the most influential families in the Middle East. They had oil money that went back a couple generations.

She was engaged to a prince at the age of six. The wedding was to be in the spring after her eighteenth birthday. Because she wanted to pursue art, her family decided to punish her.

She was to undergo female circumcision. It's rarely done on someone her age in the Middle East anymore. When she contacted Mitchell Kovich, he's my brother-in-law's friend. Mitch contacted me directly. I'd done another job for him a few years back when I was still in the forces."

She watched David lean back in his chair and realized she could imagine sitting here years from now, listening to his stories. He took another sip of his beer and when he realized it was empty, leaned over and grabbed another from the small fridge under the outside bar.

"What happened to the girl?" She leaned on the glass table; she couldn't stand the suspense.

"Oh, she's fine. She's safe somewhere in the States. It took some doing, and I don't think I'd ever try to go back into certain parts of the Middle East again, but she's healthy and happy, so my sister tells me.

She and her husband own the art galleries that sell her art. I can still remember the smile in her eyes when I showed up the night before her punishment was to take place. I was hanging from the banister outside her window, and when I showed up, she didn't even scream. It was like she was dead inside. She'd thought I'd come to kill her.

When I told her I was coming to take her to Mitch, her eyes..." He paused and Alice thought she saw something close to pride on his face. "She was wearing her hijab, the heavy, dark robes they wear, and all I could see was her eyes and I swear, I've never seen eyes light up like hers did that night.

I guess I decided then and there that this job is what I was made to do."

"You are amazing," she said then drank the last of her second drink. "Is there anything you can't do?" She smiled over at him while resting her chin on her hand.

He looked over at her and smiled slowly. "I can't seem to keep my hands off of you." She smiled back and slowly rose to her feet. Then started walking backwards towards the pool.

"Why even try?" It came out as a whisper. She saw him stand up quickly and start to follow her towards the water. She knew she wouldn't make it to the edge of the pool before he was on her.

He grabbed her around the waist as they went sailing across the empty space and landed in the deep end of the pool. Their bodies tangled, their lips found each other's and within seconds, her slick silver swimsuit was floating on the surface of the cool water.

When they surfaced again, she pulled back and had to gulp for breath. "You super-agent types may have super-sized lungs that can stay under for minutes, but us mere mortals must have air occasionally."

She smiled at him. Then he moved his hands and the smile fell away, and she was left gasping for air for another reason.

She'd never made love in a pool before and at first, she was trying to figure out just how they would accomplish the task.

As he ran his hands over her slowly, he kicked his legs until he was able to stand on the tile bottom. He moved so her back was against the pool wall and her head rested on the tiled side. She quickly pulled his shorts down and he kicked a few times before he finally got them loose from his feet.

Then, he kissed her again, his hands on either side of her head, holding her to the wall. Even though he wasn't touching her with his hands, she could feel the heat from his body as his skin rubbed against hers. Her chest rubbed against the light covering of hair on his chest, causing little tidal waves of pleasure.

Her hands ran down his slick shoulders, down his sides, until she gripped his hips and pulled him to her as she wrapped her legs around his waist. She held herself up but when her head started to sink below the surface, he grabbed her under her arms and held her tight against the wall so she wouldn't fall back down. Then with one quick motion, he sunk deep in her as she arched to greet him.

The water drank at her chest and neck as the slow motion of their bodies colliding caused little waves in the otherwise calm water. The sun felt wonderful on her face as she leaned back and enjoyed his hot kisses on her jaw and neck.

His free hand was roaming her body, giving her immense pleasure everywhere.

Her legs were still wrapped around his hips and when she tried to pull him tighter, he pulled back a little and looked at her.

When she opened her eyes, she could see something there, something she hadn't seen yet.

"I want you to meet my family in Washington." He held still, almost holding his breath. She could tell it meant a lot to him and when she nodded her head yes, he smiled and kissed her softly on the lips.

She took the kiss deeper, running her fingers through his dark hair, keeping his mouth to hers until she felt her lungs explode.

Then, she pulled back, and reaching around, took his hips, sinking her nails into his skin. She willed him to move faster. He did. He grabbed hold of the side of the pool to anchor himself as he pumped his hips until they were both breathless. Then, when she couldn't wait any longer, she felt him tense with his release, just as the stars exploded behind her eyes.

"I'm going to get you in a bed one of these times," he groaned as he buried his face in her wet hair. She smelled of chlorine and tasted like heaven. If he didn't hold them both up in the water, there was no doubt that they would sink to the bottom.

She chuckled lightly, her perfect breasts rubbing against his chest. He could already feel himself getting hard again and this time, he wanted her horizontal and on a soft surface.

Using his new-found energy, he pulled her to the wide steps and carried her to one of the large, soft recliners that sat on the wide deck. He laid her down on it, grabbed the large towel, and quickly dried himself off, shaking his head like a dog to dry his hair quickly.

Then, while she watched him, he took the towel and slowly started to dry her legs. As he traveled up each long limb, he thought he saw her desire building.

By the time he ran the edge of the towel across the height of her legs, her eyes were closed and her head was tilted back.

He couldn't pass up the chance to tease her, so he lightly passed over the spot again, watching her face as he went.

He slowly dried her stomach, making sure to hit every sensitive rib. Her hands came up, trying to pull him down until he finally gripped them in one of his hands and pulled them above her head, holding her still.

"David, please."

"I want to enjoy every inch of you. You look so beautiful in the sun. Your skin is like silk under my fingers." He leaned over and took her nipple into his mouth, sucking gently on the peak until he heard her moan.

Then he started down, raining hot kisses over her toned stomach until finally he came back to her core, where he dipped his head and tasted her sweetness. Her hands gripped his hair as she spread her legs wider on the soft cushion. He ran his hands up her legs and spread them even wider, pulling her knees up so her feet were flat beside his shoulders, exposing her even more to his mouth. Then he moved his hands to her butt and lifted her hips off the cushions, holding her tight so he could slide his tongue over her from front to back. He enjoyed licking every inch of her as her toes curled next to him.

When he was happy that she couldn't stand any more, he kissed his way up her body until he slid slowly into her. He watched as her eyes clouded and closed on a moan.

"Come with me, Alice," he said with his mouth next to hers as he claimed her, completely.

Chapter 12

Enjoying the Beach

A lice woke later in a darkened room. Reaching around and feeling the sheets, she found that she was lying in a very large bed, alone.

Sitting up, she realized she was still very naked and grabbed the sheet to cover herself as she looked around for something to wear.

She noticed a large suitcase sitting on the dresser. Walking over, she realized it was full of woman's clothing. Looking at the expensive items, she wondered how Raul had known her size, or for that matter, how he'd known that she'd be coming along.

She pulled out a silk tank top and slipped it over her head, then put on a pair of black shorts and tiptoed into the next room. She could hear him talking on the phone out on the patio and when she walked out, he turned and smiled at her.

"Yeah, okay. I'll see you then. I love you, too, Mom." He flipped the cellphone closed.

She thought it was the most endearing thing for him to tell his mother that he loved her. She hadn't realized until then that she'd totally fallen head over heels in love with him.

The realization took her breath away, and she stood there looking and feeling like an idiot. Her arms were down by her sides, feeling like weights holding her still.

Her eyes were staring off into the distance, not really seeing. How had she come to this point in her life? Sure, she'd felt infatuation before.

She'd even felt a distinct like, but nothing had ever come this close to the big fall before.

Her heart started beating faster, and she wished he'd stop staring at her. He stood there across the dimly lit deck with the bright stars and moon overhead, and they just looked at each other, almost like they had just found each other after searching for years.

"Alice?" Her name sounded good in the wind and before she knew it, she was in his arms as he carried her back into the bedroom.

The next morning, she woke to the enticing smells of bacon and eggs and stretched on the large bed. She realized she was once again naked and smiled.

Grabbing up her top and shorts, she walked into the next room and laughed as she saw him standing at the stove with an apron on.

"Is this what you always wear to cook in, in your glass house?" She chuckled as he turned a circle and showed her the front of his apron which had a large picture of a woman's front in a string bikini. He held the spatula up and smiled at her, looking ridiculous.

"Only on Monday's. Okay, it's Raul's, but it's kind of growing on me." He looked down and chuckled at his image, then looked back up at her and waved his finger at her.

"Why don't you come over here and kiss the cook."

She walked over and laid a long, heated kiss on him.

"Mmmm, why don't we forget the food and…" He started walking her back to the bedroom.

"Oh no! That food smells too good to pass up. Besides, we have the whole day to…" She kissed him again.

She enjoyed sitting out on the deck and eating breakfast with him. This morning they kept the conversation light.

After they had cleaned the dishes, they decided a quick trip to the beach and town would help pass their time quickly.

Besides, she'd never been to this island and wanted to have a look around before they had to hop back on another plane tomorrow.

In the back of her mind, she kept dreading being shoved into another crate and carted to the US. Even though she didn't know if that was how they were going to travel, she doubted they'd get first class seats since they were trying to lay low.

They drove a small Audi that had been parked in the garage into town and when she asked, he said he kept it around for Raul to use. She started wondering how much he earned by being a mercenary.

When they finally made it into town, she was too preoccupied by all the wonderful shops and stores to think about what he did for a living. It was almost as if she was back in the US.

The shops and tall glass buildings made her feel a little more like she was home. The fact that everyone spoke Spanish didn't escape her, though. She'd spent a few years taking the language in school and felt almost at ease speaking it. She purchased a new handbag and some new boots at the small stores thanks to David, who had quickly paid for the items in cash.

She told him on the short ride to the beach that she'd pay him back, he just smiled.

When they made it to the white sand beach, she knew exactly why he'd chosen to buy a place here. The beaches were more beautiful than any resort she'd ever been to. The sand and water sparkled, and the people smiled and were very friendly.

They spent almost two hours playing on the surf. He even taught her how to body surf. She was a complete failure at it but enjoyed having his hands on her while he taught her how to lay her body flat to catch the surf.

By the time they made it back to the house, she was worn out. David walked into the next room to check his messages and came back in holding the phone and looking worried.

"Your father called. He wants you to call him as soon as possible." He handed her the phone. "Don't worry, it's a secure line. No one can trace the call." When she took the phone, he turned and walked out, shutting the door quietly behind him.

In the last few days, she hadn't really thought of what her father must be going through. She thought that since David had talked to Steve that first day, her father knew that she was okay. Other than that, he'd been so far from her mind.

She started feeling guilty. Okay, so she'd been running for her life. It wasn't as if she'd had time to think of him. Then her mind played over last night and today she felt even more guilty.

She should have called him last night when she'd heard David talking to his mother. Damn.

Dialing the phone, she waited as it rang. On the third ring, Blake picked up the phone. Hearing his husky voice, she almost cried. To think he'd gone through something like this just five years ago.

"Hey, Blake. How are you doing?" She tried to sound lighthearted.

"Hey, Alice. Dad and Mom were just talking about you. I guess you got in some trouble, huh?"

"Yeah, but everything is okay and we're on our way back home."

"Is GI Joe with you?"

"Yeah," she smiled.

"Cool, tell him hi from me. Here's dad. He's pretty upset that you didn't call him last night."

Her heart sank a little and she listened as her brother handed the phone over.

"Hey, Alice. Is everything okay?"

"Yeah, Dad. I'm sorry I didn't call you sooner. I guess I've kind of been in shock with everything that's happened over the last few days."

She hated lying to her father, but doubted he would want to hear all the details of her sex life.

"Listen, the real reason I needed to talk to you was that I have some news as to why you might be in trouble."

He let the phone ring until finally, on the fourth ring, the man answered.

"They are in Guatemala."

"Guatemala? Are you sure? I can have my men…"

"Don't bother, they won't be there long. They are heading back to the States.

I need you here."

"Okay, give me a few hours to round up some men."

"No, for what I have in mind, all we will need is you. Too many men will draw attention. This is going to be a more personal setting and I think someone with your skills will be just what we need."

"What kind of equipment shall I bring?"

"Nothing. I'll arrange everything you will need here. There might even be a way that you can redeem yourself for letting Alice slip through your fingers in Ponce. Just get here as quickly as you can."

After he hung up, he sat in the dark room and thought about the new plan.

Letting her come home might not be the best plan, but having her close and having the possibility of personally getting his hands on her thrilled him.

He'd wanted his hands on her since the first time he'd been introduced to her by her father. Being close to the family was a blessing. Hiding in plain sight had always been his specialty.

Now, he just needed to spin his web so he could sit back and wait for them to take the bait.

He thought of all the hard work he'd done over the last year, all the lies, all the deception, and smiled. He was good at his job. He'd surrounded himself so far in society that if he disappeared, it wouldn't go unnoticed. Plus, he was in too good of a position to not be an asset.

The goal was the same, to stop the senator at any cost. So much money was riding on him doing his job well. Drug money ran through his veins. It was what drove him and the people he worked for.

Power and wealth had become something easily obtained if you knew the right people and didn't mind getting your hands dirty.

He looked down at his manicured fingers and smiled knowing his hands were dirtier than most others. Just because he enjoyed the job, it didn't mean he didn't have the drive to someday be the one calling all the shots.

He knew his boss wasn't pleased that it had taken this long, but what could the old man does. It wasn't like the man was around much anyway. When he was there, though, he was a force to be reckoned with.

He was one step away from taking over. After all, the old man was very old and frail. He couldn't live forever. Maybe after this job was over, he'd have to personally step in and see the man's health. He knew a few tricks for helping someone's health deteriorate. It wasn't as if he couldn't get close to the man. He was a lone wolf after all.

Yes, it would be nice to not have to worry about doing someone else's dirty work. He leaned back in the chair and crossed his arms behind his head. Looking around the dark office, he could just imagine it all being his one day.

After hanging up the phone with her father, Alice walked back into the living room feeling lightheaded. She found David at the table on a laptop and talking on another phone.

He looked busy, so she sat and zoned out while he talked. She was so busy thinking about the conversation she'd just had with her father, that when David came and sat next to her, she almost jumped.

"Sorry, I know you were deep in thought. I didn't mean to startle you."

"It's not my fault. The interview had nothing to do with what happened in Ponce," she blurted out.

"Yeah. I just confirmed that, as well. It appears there's a contract out on you.

They're after your father for his new bill that will make it harder for drugs to come into the US through Texas. Alice."

He waited until she turned and looked at him. "That's why he hired me. Just in case this was going to come back to him, through you. My buddy Marco is watching Blake. I have some of my other buddies watching your family back home. I knew it could be something like this, but I wasn't sure."

He ran his hands through his hair, and she could tell he was struggling. "I guess I should have told you. I didn't think."

"You knew there was a chance that all this," she said, waving her hands in the air wildly, "wasn't my fault and you didn't say anything?"

She stood and looked down at him. The hurt and guilt she'd felt since seeing her friend's body replayed in her mind. He could have spared her some of that. She walked from the room, heading out the glass doors towards the cliffs. When she reached the edge, she sat down in the grass and cried.

When the sun started sinking below the water, David walked out and sat next to her. His arms rested on his knees as he looked off towards the sunset.

"Alice, there's a lot about me that I haven't told you. A lot of things I don't want to tell you. A lot of things I can't tell you."

He turned and looked at her. "If I kept something from you, it was for a reason. I didn't know for sure it had anything to do with your father. I was under the same assumption as you were, that it had everything to do with this." He pulled the black disk from his pocket and set it in her lap.

"Ivan sent a copy to Austin the morning after everything exploded. This is just your copy."

"You had this, the entire time?" She looked at him. When he nodded, she felt even more betrayed.

"Don't," he said and pulled her shoulders until she looked at him. "What I did, everything I did, was to protect you. You didn't trust me when we first started this journey. I didn't trust you. I needed that leverage over you, in case you tried to bolt. You were safer with me, and I needed you to have a reason to stay."

She looked down at the disk in her hands and remembered thinking about getting him fired from his job. Then she realized he was making sense.

"What about now?" She looked at him and saw the confusion in his eyes.

"You obviously trust me enough to give me this. Do you think I'll take off?"

"I hope you won't for more reasons than I'm willing to admit to right now."

He looked back towards the sunset and pulled her into his arms. "I still want you to come to Washington, to meet my family." He kissed the top of her head, "But I'd totally understand if you didn't."

She sighed and thought about it, then leaned onto his shoulder even more.

"David, I trust you completely. I'd still love to go with you to meet your family."

They sat there watching the sun set together and she knew without a doubt that she'd fallen hard for him. There was no way she would ever turn back.

Chapter 13

The Escape

That night David didn't get much sleep. The fact that he never really slept the whole night through didn't normally bother him. That night he wanted nothing more than to lay there holding Alice and dozing off peacefully.

His mind just wouldn't shut down, so he gently moved her off his chest and went into the living room to work on his laptop. He checked their travel arrangements and chatted online with his contacts. Then he emailed his sister, Roberta, and told her they were going to be in town.

He checked the news in Ponce and checked in with his sources there. When he got in touch with Ivan, he was shocked to hear that he'd had to disappear for a while and was now back in Jamaica.

Evidently word had gotten out that he'd helped them escape, and he was blacklisted around Ponce. So, he'd hightailed it back home to lay low. He'd ended up doing some more research on Alice's father. Trying to find out who was after him was like finding a needle in a haystack.

There were too many drug lords out there that would want to see the Senator's new bill fail. Just as the sun was rising, David walked in and woke Alice so they could start their journey to the States.

By the time they were showered and dressed, Raul was driving up to the house and they loaded their new luggage filled with their new clothes in the back of the van.

"No crate this time?" Alice asked as they sat in the back of the plush van.

David laughed.

"No, this time we ride in style."

The private jet left the small airport less than an hour later. Its pilot another one of David's trusted buddies from his Special Forces days.

"I could get used to this," Alice said, leaning back in the leather chair. The private cabin was not only plush but packed with a few extra benefits as well.

The gourmet food brought out by the flight attendant was of the highest quality.

"Okay," Alice asked after eating baked salmon and fresh vegetables, "who did you must rescue to use this?"

He just chuckled and shook his head. "If I told you, I'd have to kill you." He leaned over and kissed her nose as she pouted.

This flight seemed to go a lot faster than the one they'd taken a few days ago.

Maybe because this time they talked and enjoyed each other's company, which always seemed to make the time fly by. He just couldn't keep his eyes from her face as she talked about her life and family.

Her eyes seemed to sparkle when she talked about her little brother, who was almost half her age. He did see some hesitation when she talked about her stepmother, Coleen.

She didn't go into detail about the woman, but David had met her once already. He remembered a very tan, toned, young woman who had hugged him excessively to thank him for returning her son.

Her jet-black hair had matched that of the young boy's. It hadn't escaped David's notice that the young boy had held onto his father longer than his mother.

Alice seemed to enjoy talking about her life and career choices. David thought she was making up for lost time in getting to know each other, or maybe it was just nervous chatter.

He knew he felt a little nervous about bringing her to meet his family. After all, he'd never brought someone home before, ever.

He was pretty sure at one point his father had just assumed he was gay. He'd laughed about it then, but it had made him start to wonder if he'd ever find someone he'd want to bring home.

Looking over at Alice, again, he realized there was no doubt in his mind that she was the one. He knew his parents would accept her immediately.

After all, they had taken Roberta in with open arms after she'd visited them for the first time a few years back. It was the first time his mother had seen her daughter since she was a few days old. Meeting your son's girlfriend seemed like a much smaller step than finding your long-lost daughter.

He felt the plane slowing and starting its descent.

"I haven't been to Portland before. I've been to Seattle, but never to Oregon," Alice said, sounding eager as she leaned to get a better look out the window.

"Oh my God!" she said and turned so her shoulders were facing the window. Her hands went to either side of the small window. "Is that Mt. Hood?

It's so close and big."

He chuckled. Most people flying into Portland for the first time had the same thought. He looked out his window and seeing the large, white peak hovering over the city made him feel like he was home. He missed it. He missed his family. He missed just relaxing and not being on the run. Looking over at Ann, he realized she was the reason.

"Yes, it's over eleven thousand feet. Isn't it beautiful?"

She turned and smiled at him. "Where is it you're from again?"

"Cathlamet, Washington. It's a very small town about an hour and a half from Portland. We'll spend the night at my sister Roberta's place in town tonight. Then we'll drive over tomorrow to visit my folks and my grandma."

When the plane finished taxiing, the doors were opened, and he smiled as the cool air hit him in the face. The smell of home made him want to close his eyes and take it all in.

After getting their luggage, they grabbed a taxi and less than thirty minutes later were walking up to his sister's front door. The newer stone home was in an older part of town, and he knew they'd just finished renovating the whole thing.

It was where they stayed while they were in town, but their larger full-time home was in a small town called Cattles almost two hours away.

As they approached, the blue front door swung open and a small girl with dark hair came running towards them.

"David," she said repeatedly. He laughed and pulled her up into a tight hug. She'd grown so much since he'd seen her four months ago. Her little chubby cheeks were still kissable. When she started talking, he noticed a few more teeth in her mouth.

"How's my Rose-petal?" He swung her in a circle and kissed her all over her face, causing her to giggle.

He looked over and saw his sister and brother-in-law, Ric, standing in the front doorway. His sister walked up and gave him a hug. He kissed the top of her dark head while still holding Rose. Rose was lucky enough to have gotten the best of both of her parents. Her big blue eyes she'd gotten from her dad. Her long dark hair and cute button nose she'd gotten from her mother.

"Alice, this is my sister Roberta and her husband Ric. This," he tickled the little girl in his arms, "This is my Rose-petal." The girl giggled and he watched Alice smile and shake his sister's hand, then Ric's.

Alice felt a little overwhelmed. He had told her about his sister, that she was an ex-detective. The thing that really loomed over Alice's mind was the fact that Roberta had been stolen as a child and raised by a thief.

She didn't know exactly what had turned her life around, but she knew that Roberta had become a cop early on. After retiring young she'd become head of security for her husband who owned one of the largest growing franchises of art galleries in the US.

The couple was nothing like she had imagined. They were both fit and very tan, almost like they spent more time outside than inside.

Guessing the number of clouds she'd seen on the short taxi ride over here, she doubted they got so tan from the sun around here.

She could see some similarity between Roberta and David. They had matching eyes and hair. Roberta was very petite and a whole lot shorter. Ric was tall and blonde, and his smile was almost infectious as he chatted with David.

Their townhouse was gorgeous. Its tall ceilings and light tan walls made her feel almost at home. David carried their luggage up to the room they'd be staying in while Alice excused herself and freshened up in the small powder bathroom.

She'd never had a problem talking with people before, but for some reason, it really mattered to her what this couple thought of her. She tried to be smooth around them, but her nerves were showing.

Finally, Roberta pulled her aside and asked for her help in the kitchen.

Alice looked around the large kitchen as the men talked in the living room area.

Roberta was just putting the finishing touches on a big pan of lasagna while Alice finished fixing the salad.

"You know, I didn't meet my brother until a few years ago, but that doesn't mean I don't love him."

Alice looked over at Roberta. The woman was leaning against the countertop, her arms crossed over her chest as she watched her finishing the salad.

"I understand. I have a half-brother that's half my age. I can't stand his mother, but the kid just gets to me."

She smiled, thinking of Blake's face. Roberta smiled. "You know, Alice, I think I like you. It was hard to tell at first. There's just something about reporters that gets under my skin. But you…"

Roberta nodded her head. "There's this realness underneath it all that I've never seen in one of your kind before."

Alice laughed. "One of my kind. I like that. I've never been associated as a "Kind" before."

Roberta laughed. "You know, when I worked the force, I thought of your kind as a bunch of zombies, sucking the stories from the humans by any means possible."

They both laughed as they carried the food into the dining room.

Alice couldn't get over how comfortable David was around Rose. The little two-year-old hung on him and when her little head started nodding off after dinner, he gently carried her upstairs and was gone for a while.

After their talk in the kitchen, Alice had relaxed around Ric and Roberta, so the conversations flowed at a comfortable pace.

She learned all about his sister's childhood, how she'd grown up in a gang, how she'd become a detective. The way Roberta told the story, Alice could just imagine it all happening and felt even more respect for the woman sitting in front of her.

She loved hearing the adventure Ric and Roberta had gone through together a few years back. How it had all been caused because of Ric's friend Mitchell, when he'd asked David to bring Sandi to America.

"Actually," David said looking at his sister, "the first day I saw you in Portland, I was at the hospital that day because of that case. I'd just brought Sandi into the US. How we got here? That's another story, but I'd just dropped her off at the safe point when Ivan, who was working the case with me, got sick. Appendicitis."

He chuckled remembering how the big man had been taken down so quickly by the pains.

"You know, in a roundabout way if it wasn't for you, Rob and I would have never met." Ric smiled at his wife.

"Yeah, thanks little brother. You do remember I was shot near the end there."

"I know," David looked sad. "You scared us all."

"Was it worth it?" Alice asked over her glass of wine.

"Yes, I did get my man." She smiled and snuggled closer to her husband's side on the couch.

When Alice was lying next to David a few hours later, she rolled over and looked at him, resting her chin in her hands on his chest.

"I like your sister and her family. I can't believe everything she's gone through in life."

He smiled at her and continued to run his hand down her hair. "I can tell she likes you, too."

"Really?" She sat up a little more, looking into his face.

He nodded and smiled. "She didn't kick you out of her house. Rob is a really simple person. If she likes you, you're in. If she doesn't, there would have been no doubt about her feelings and you would have found yourself sleeping in the alley."

She smiled; she couldn't help it. Roberta was her kind of girl.

Where was she? He'd been told that she was heading straight home, days ago. He was usually a patient man, but waiting this long for something was wearing him thin.

He tried to get more information from her family, but no one was talking.

He'd even sent his man into her work to see if someone would tell them where she'd disappeared to.

His boss was getting agitated. His plans kept changing and he had to justify all his moves. Reasoning everything out was just a waste of his time.

He thought of Alice and remembered the first time he'd been introduced to her. Her long blond hair had caught his attention right away. She was as tall as he was and he found that very attractive. Her legs were skinny, and he knew he'd enjoy running his hands up them. He felt himself hardening thinking of her.

"Are you coming back to bed?" A rich female voice broke into his thoughts.

Looking up he saw the brunette standing naked across his small office in the rented house. Her long dark legs were crossed as she leaned against the door frame. She still wore her black heels and stockings.

Her perky breast peaked upwards, and he knew they tasted just like the name she went by, Cinnamon. He didn't mind paying for a good time and tonight's treat had been one he'd enjoyed many times over the last few months. His mind was now running to a certain blond.

Maybe he could use the energy he had pent up for Alice and enjoy one last night with Cinnamon before his job was done here.

Standing up, he walked over and grabbed her by the waist and bent her over the desk so that her face lay on the cool surface. He dropped his pants and plunged into her in one quick motion.

Closing his eyes, he dreamed of seeing the blond hair pooling around the wood of his desk as he pounded her until he felt his release explode.

Chapter 14

David Visiting His Parents

The next morning, after eating a huge breakfast and saying goodbye to Rob, Ric, and Rose, Alice and David settled in their rental car for the hour-and-half journey to see his parents.

She watched the scenery change outside of town and the houses started getting further apart and smaller. Green fields covered most of the landscape and the trees were thicker.

By the time they turned off and drove through the town of Longview, she could feel her nerves building again. Shortly after they'd made it through the town, she lost herself in the drive again.

The road narrowed to a small two lane, and she couldn't remember seeing a drive more peaceful or relaxing. Several times she would get a peek at the large river, the Columbia, which sat just beside the winding road.

The drive seemed to go on and she realized that they had hadn't even passed any towns for a while.

"Here we are," David said as they pulled into a small side road which led down towards the small town. She could see the small cottages that lined the streets. The river was right there, and she could see a small dock area that housed a few dozen boats of all shapes and sizes.

"My parents live in the house just up there, and my house is up that way as well, but we're heading over to my grandmother's place first. She's lived there her whole life.

My grandpa died when I was seventeen in an accident at the mill. He would have liked you." He smiled at her as he drove up a steep hill and stopped in front of a small wood framed house with a red roof.

Potted plants hung on the quaint front porch, and large pots of bright flowers sat everywhere. An older woman sat on the porch and when their car stopped, she stood up and waved.

"My grandma, Eliza. She'll like you, too. I suppose my folks are running late. My dad never could be on time for anything."

Alice watched as David surrounded his grandmother in a hug. She could see the love between the two instantly, making her wish she'd had more time with her own grandmother before she passed away.

"You must be Alice. It's such a pleasure to meet you, dear." The woman hugged her lightly and smiled at David. "Please, I have some tea ready, would you like to sit?"

Just as they made it to the front porch, a white truck pulled up and honked.

"Oh good, your parents are finally here."

Alice watched as a man roughly the size of David exited the truck and walked over to open the door for a woman who was the spitting image of her daughter, Roberta.

When they approached, she could see small differences, but there was no doubt left in Alice's mind as to how knew who Roberta that day was at the hospital.

David, on the other hand, took after his father more. Their builds were identical and Alice was impressed with the amount of muscle on his father. She wondered if they ever bragged about whose were bigger.

Smiling, she shook their hands after David introduced them. Of course, they'd both come in and given her hugs, making her feel very welcomed.

An hour later, Alice couldn't imagine laughing any harder. His mother was telling her all kinds of stories about David when he was a child.

David, for his part, sat there and just laughed or smiled back. She couldn't imagine him coming from this kind of family and doing what he did for a living.

She'd always thought that soldiers were hardened, raised in rough families. Like they were searching for an out and found it by doing what they did. It made him a bigger puzzle than she'd thought.

She'd never really asked him why he did what he did if there had been any one reason he'd chosen his career. She could tell that he kept most of the stuff he did away from his family. From what she could gather, they thought of him as kind of a security guard.

After dinner, they finally headed out to his place. He'd mentioned he had a house in town near his parents' place, but what he hadn't mentioned is that he had built it himself.

They drove up the long driveway as a light, steady rain fell. She'd made a comment about how beautiful it was, and he'd confided that it had taken him and his father a whole year to finish it.

The wood cabin look was stunning. The large front porch wrapped around the entire place and there were at least two swings hanging from the porch.

When he pulled the car around back, she noticed the large three-car carport attached to the garage.

"My father stores his tractor in the garage. They watch the place while I'm away. Their house is just there." He pointed across a huge field. "You can see the lights." She looked and, indeed, about a mile across the field she could see house lights. ", they own all the land. I bought this small chunk from them. Well, he wouldn't let me pay for it." He smiled.

"It's beautiful."

"Wait till you see inside." He grabbed her hand and walked her in the door.

She noticed it wasn't locked and stopped.

"Alice, this is small-town Washington. No one locks their doors. The worst we must deal with is deer eating our crops, and raccoons or bears getting into our trash."

She looked around quickly for prowling bears as he laughed. They walked in the back door which led them straight into a large kitchen. The steel stove sat in the middle on an island with a large steel vent hood over it.

Large pots hung by a rack on either side of the vent. The marble countertops were a cream color matching the light oak cabinets. The tile floor in olive green and beige gave it all a warm feeling. There was a small kitchen table and chairs off to the left near a large glass window which overlooked the fields.

As they walked through the place, David talked about the construction and how he and his father had worked together. It was the most he'd said since she'd met him. She enjoyed hearing every detail.

The living room was off to the left and as she took the two steps into the sunken space, she marveled at the large two-story stone fireplace. The massive moose head that hung over it was just as impressive.

"My uncle got him in Alaska. He gave it to me as a birthday gift. I've been hunting with him a few times. Got myself a black bear once." He smiled. "But fishing is more to my taste. I know the perfect spot to get some great salmon.

Maybe next year..." he broke off and took her hand. "Well, how about I finish showing you around?"

She nodded her head. She didn't know what else to say. He'd hinted at their relationship continuing. Did that mean she wasn't just a job? But he'd broken his statement off. Did that mean he'd regretted saying it? Ugh! She hated having doubts.

They climbed a twisted staircase with shiny wood railings up to a landing.

There she stopped and looked down at the living space. She could really enjoy the view of the large fireplace from here. There were large windows on either side and she could just make out the river in the distance.

"How often do you get to stay here?"

"Well, I try to make it home for the whole holiday season. The last few years, since I've been working alone, it's been easier for me to schedule my time so, I make sure I'm here more often. I don't get to stay as often as I'd like."

They walked into a large bedroom that had a mini version of the fireplace along the inside wall. The bed was huge, most likely a California king.

She looked at David and realized he'd need a large bed to be comfortable in. The bed in his Guatemala home had been large, but not this large. She'd noticed his feet hung off it and thought that in this bed, he'd have room to spare.

"We built it with three bedrooms upstairs. I have a gym downstairs and an office."

She walked over and sat on the bed.

"I'm impressed. You did such a wonderful job." She smiled at him as he walked across the room. She could feel the heat from his stare burning into her skin.

"I've wanted to see you here. In my home. In my bed."

She smiled at him and held her arms up for him. He leaned in and kissed her mouth, pulling them both down onto the soft bed.

He rained slow kisses over her face and neck as she arched back and wrapped her legs around his hips, her hands slowly pulling his shirt up and over his head.

She could hear the rain hitting the roof, and the soothing sounds and the dim light from the windows made her want to go slow. She had all night to show him what she'd been feeling. To show him how much she wanted him, wanted to be with him here.

Once his shirt was removed, she ran her hands over his skin, enjoying the muscles as she watched them flex and jump under her fingers.

"Mmmm, I love your body." She leaned up and kissed his collar bone, running her tongue over him, tasting him.

She used her hands and pushed his shoulders until he was lying flat on his back, shirtless. She straddled his hips and slowly removed her shirt, watching his eyes heat as he watched her.

"I love seeing what I do to you. Seeing your eyes focus on me." She slowly ran her hands over her skin until she came to her black bra. Then she leaned down and ran her fingers over his chest, running a finger down his stomach, down the pathway below his belly button until she hit the clasp of his jeans.

She unbuttoned, then slowly unzipped them. His arms flexed as he put his hands above his head, resting his head in his palms. He smiled at her, giving her permission to do what she wanted with him. She couldn't help it, she smiled back.

"You are in so much trouble." She moved down so she could slowly pull his jeans off his hips. When she got to his boots, she took her time unlacing them and pulling them off one at a time. She knew the anticipation was killing him.

Several times he tried to help her, but she just pushed his hands aside.

Finally, when he was lying beneath her naked, she just looked down at him.

She was still half dressed in her black bra and black skirt. Her thigh-high stockings were visible as she hiked her skirt so she could straddle him again.

She'd toed off her own heels as she walked her way back to just below his hips.

His erection sat between them, proud and erect. She knew he wanted her to touch him, but she leaned over and started kissing and rubbing her hands over his chest again.

She wanted this to last. She wanted to enjoy every inch of him, slowly.

"Alice, you're killing me."

"Don't rush me. I'm enjoying myself too much to go fast." She smiled as she nibbled her way down his chest. When she reached his belly button, she dipped her tongue in and swirled it around the sexy spot. He had a light covering of hair that trailed down to his sex.

She followed it until finally, she gripped him lightly in her hands. She watched as his eyes closed and he moaned while arching his head.

"You like it when I touch you?"

"God, yes!" He almost jumped when she swirled her tongue around the head, lapping at him as she used her hands to stroke his length. She cupped his balls as she used her mouth to please him.

His hands plunged into her hair, holding her to him as she took her time enjoying the taste and feel of him in her mouth.

"Alice!" His hips were pumping, making her motion deeper and longer. Then he was quickly reversing their positions.

"You little hellcat." He smiled down at her. "Do you know what it is that you do to me?"

He looked down at her, his hands slowly going up her stockings. "I think it's time for a little payback." He smiled and she knew she was in trouble.

His calloused hands finally reached the sensitive skin above her thigh-highs.

He slowly rolled each stocking down until finally her legs were bare. Then he dipped his head and kissed and licked his way back up her legs until finally he reached the inside of her thighs.

Her skirt was hiked up, exposing her silk panties, but he made no move to remove them. Instead, as his eyes were on hers, he reached up and undid her bra, slowly pulling it down her shoulders.

Her hands were beside her on the bed and when he'd finally finished removing it, she gripped the bedspread and wished for speed. How could she know that moving so slow would tie her up inside?

"David, please." She watched as he smiled.

"Shh, don't rush me. I'm enjoying myself too much to go fast." He repeated her words, tormenting her.

With just his fingers, he trailed over her soft skin until he circled her nipples, causing them to rise and bud. Then he just looked down at her. "Beautiful." He smiled, then dipped his head to taste the skin he'd just exposed.

She arched up and grabbed his hair as he rained wet kisses over her heated skin.

He trailed kisses down until he reached the top of her skirt. Then he moved back down below to the inside of her thighs again.

She felt like she couldn't breathe, waiting for him to touch her in the place she wanted, the place she needed him. Slowly, he ran his hands up until he could pull her silk panties down her legs slowly.

Then he ran his mouth over her heated skin, moving upwards until, finally, his mouth licked her tender skin causing her to arch off the bed and moan.

He used his hands to hike her skirt higher, pushing it up until she was fully exposed. He dipped his head as he used his hands to spread her legs wider, exposing her fully to his view and taste.

He ran his hands up her inner thigh until he slid a finger into her core while his tongue pleasured her skin. Her shoulders came off the mattress then as she screamed his name.

"Mmm." He trailed kisses up her stomach and she realized every muscle in her body was totally relaxed. "I could get used to this," he said when he was fully on top of her, his chest and hips pinning her to the mattress. He used his thighs to spread her legs until he fit comfortably between them. "Ann?" She smiled and opened her eyes.

His face was close, so close she had to blink a few times to adjust her eyes.

His eyes sparkled in the dim light, and she noticed a huge smile on his face.

"I want to see what I do to you when I slide into you. I want to see your eyes as I drive you over the edge."

He paused as he slid slowly into her. She tried to keep her eyes focused on him, but she couldn't help that everything had gone blurry. She gripped his shoulders as he slowly rocked his hips.

She could feel his speed pick up as his hips pumped harder and faster. She closed her eyes to the pleasure and wrapped her legs around his hips to hold on.

Finally, when she couldn't stand it another minute, he buried his face into her hair and let himself go just as she fell.

The thin man was sweating. Even though the room's temperature was controlled at a cool seventy degrees, he felt it dripping down his back. His palms were sweaty and he knew that his heart was racing.

"I assure you I will be dealing with this situation myself. I have my top man here in town, ready to take the shot at a minute's notice. I have some big plans to finally remove the senator. I still have one more opportunity to deal with his daughter that I'd like to try."

"You don't even know where the girl is now."

"I know she'll be back in town in a few days. I've just found out where she is and thought it would be better to wait until she was back in Austin before making my move."

"You thought? I wasn't aware I paid you to think. Your job is to do what I tell you to. Nothing more. I told you to get the girl in Rio. Did you get the girl in Ponce like I requested?"

"No, she slipped through our fingers. I've explained."

"I don't want to hear any more excuses. Do you know how important it is that Senator Rhodes drops from this race?"

He nodded his head and dropped his eyes from the old man's face to the floor.

"I don't want to be mad at you. You've been my right hand for how many years now?"

"Four, sir."

"Has it been that long?" The old man looked down at his watch.

"Well, when Miss Rhodes gets back in town, I want you to make sure you take care of everything. If you can't get to the girl, don't waste your time. I want that speech stopped at any cost. Am I making myself clear?"

"Yes, sir."

The old man stood and grabbed his briefcase. "Well...? Get out of my office.

I'm running late for a meeting. Oh, and I don't want to see you again until after everything is taken care of."

Chapter 15

David In Love

The next morning, they met his parents for a day trip to the beach, something they'd done since he was a kid. Usually, they'd spend the whole night sleeping in a tent or sleeping bags under the stars if the weather held out.

This time they had stayed late enough to have some of his dad's homemade mussel soup. He laughed as he taught Alice how to dig for mussels.

She'd been a little grossed out at first, but after he'd showed her how to collect the first few, she'd rolled her sleeves up and been totally focused.

She'd even helped him collect wood for their fire. He'd always enjoyed having a campfire on the beach. Something about the smell of burning wood and the salt from the ocean made him feel like he was truly home.

As they sat on a large piece of driftwood in front of the fire, he pulled her close as he watched his parents laughing about a story they were telling.

It was almost like life was going in slow motion for a few minutes. His mind flashed from seeing the same scene as a child, to seeing them now, and then for a moment, he could just imagine how they would look years from now. Still laughing. Still sitting close and holding hands.

He'd wanted what they had his whole life. The connection they shared went beyond the title of husband and wife. It was even beyond the word friendship.

He supposed if he had to choose a word for what his parents had together it would be perfection.

Smiling, he looked over at Alice and at that moment, he knew he'd found his perfection. Her eyes were sparkling in the fire, and he could see that her cheeks and nose were pink from the cold wind coming off the Pacific.

Her hair was tied in a tail that hung from the back of one of his old ball caps. She was wearing one of his hunting jackets that was three sizes too big for her. Her jeans were rolled up past her ankles, so they didn't get wet on the sand. Her feet were bare, and he smiled, realizing she'd yet to repaint her toenails.

He couldn't imagine her looking better than she did right then. He didn't care if he never saw her in the hot red outfit that she'd worn the day he'd met her. He knew he'd hold onto this moment for the rest of his life.

Years from now, when his children asked him what his favorite memory was, he'd tell them it was sitting under the stars with your mother and grandparents, laughing about some silly stories and realizing how much I loved your mother.

Of course, the only thing left for him to do was tell Alice how he felt. This he wasn't so good at. He'd never told anyone he loved them before, expect his grandparents and parents.

Telling a woman, you loved her was a lot different than telling your family.

At least he thought it would be. Maybe he needed to buy her flowers? Maybe he'd just shout it out from the rooftops. Maybe he'd tell her after making love to her?

Whatever his intentions, he knew he had to think of something soon. He needed to work up the courage to tell her before they left to go back to Austin. If he didn't find the courage before then; he knew he might never find it.

It seemed their visit of two days was over too quickly. They made the journey back to Portland, and this time they hopped on a commercial plane heading towards Austin.

The fact that a few days earlier she'd been running for her life didn't escape her. Alice sat in the plane, looking at the flat landscape below her and thinking about everything she'd gone through and how her life would fall back into its normal pattern in the next few days.

Was David going to stick around? Was she still just a job to him? So many other questions ran through her head that by the time the plane landed, she had worked herself into quite a large headache.

They'd had such a wonderful time together at his place. The nights had been filled with love, the days with his family. They'd gone to the beach and she'd enjoyed mussel hunting.

Then they had sat on the beach until the evening when his father had cooked the mussels into a stew over an open fire, something she'd never tried before.

By the last day there, she was beginning to feel so comfortable around his family. His mother had even programmed her number into Alice's new cell phone. They'd taken pictures of everyone on the beach and Alice had one on her new phone of David and her kissing with the sunset behind them. She kept sneaking looks at it when he wasn't looking.

Their last night there was much like their first, but with a lot less talking. She didn't know what to say to him. They were heading back to her home. Would he want to stay? Did she want him to stay? How could she get him to stay?

He was an adventurer. He traveled everywhere. Saved countless people. Got shot at on a regular basis. Why would he want to stay? What did she really have that he'd want?

These questions kept running through her mind. So much that she'd become very withdrawn and quiet. She knew there was an awkward silence between them, but she really did need some time to think.

She knew she was being extra quiet on the long taxi ride to her condo in Georgetown, thirty minutes from Austin.

David sat quietly beside her. Most likely he was trying to figure out what to do next. She had no clue what to do, herself. By the time they had exited the taxi, she'd made up her mind that she did want him to stay. So, the only question remaining was how to convince him.

When she walked into her place, she still felt uneasy about how to tell him that she wanted him to stay. She walked around turning on the lights, and when she noticed the light on her answering machine, she walked over and hit the button, hoping it would fill in the quiet that was hanging around the room.

"Alice, it's Anthony. I need to talk to you the second you get back."

Great! she thought. She hadn't thought about the repercussions of everything with her job. She wondered suddenly if she still had a job.

She looked over at David and decided that call could wait until tomorrow.

The next message was from her father. He too wanted her to call him the second she went into town.

Picking up her phone, she hit speed dial for her dad's cell number and waited for him to pick up.

"Hey, sweetie," he answered, sounding as if he was in the car. "I didn't know what time you would be coming back into town, but we're on our way there to see you. We should be there in about ten minutes."

She looked over at David and sheer panic flooded her eyes. How was she going to explain their relationship to her father? It was one thing meeting his family, but her father knew what he was, had hired him. Would her dad welcome him like his family had done to her.

"Alice, are you still there?" Her father's voice shook her out of all the questions she'd been tossing around in her head. She blinked and turned her back on David then walked into her bedroom to finish the awkward call with her dad.

She needed to tell her dad exactly what she felt towards David so he wouldn't be shocked, or worse, try to hit David for taking advantage of her.

When she walked back out of her room, David was standing by the door with his hand on the handle.

"I know your family is on their way here, so I'll just let myself out." He turned to go.

"Wait, you don't have to go. I was just..."

"Listen, Princess, I know what you were just doing. I'm sorry. I thought..." he shook his head. "I have some loose ends to tie up.

I'll see you around. I'm still on the job, remember."

He turned and walked out without another word to her. She felt like crying, but instead, she walked into the kitchen and took a few aspirins and a glass of water, then waited for her family to get there.

When her father arrived, she'd been hugged and yelled at all at the same time. She tried not to laugh, really. But after what she'd been through, she doubted anything her father could say or do would scare her ever again.

Coleen sat on her couch quietly, checking her cell phone like she was bored.

Blake had hugged her and then after their father was almost done yelling at her, had asked so many questions about David.

"Where is he? I thought he was going to be here."

"You just missed him." She tried not to sound too depressed that he wasn't there, but when her father's eyebrows shot up, she knew that he knew something was up.

Blake proceeded to blast her with question after question as her father watched her very carefully. Finally, just before they were ready to leave, her father pulled her aside into the kitchen to talk alone.

"Okay, sweetie. Spill."

"What?" She'd tried to hide it from him all evening, but knew she hadn't done a good job.

When he just crossed his arms over his chest and looked at her, she walked over and gave him a hug. His arms came around her and she lost it. Crying on her father's shoulder was one of those things she never got too old to do.

It took almost ten minutes for her to cry herself dry. When she had, he leaned back and handed her a tissue from the box on her countertop.

"Tell me what this is all about."

"I think I screwed up." He looked at her. "It has nothing to do with what happened in Ponce. I think I screwed up with David.

Dad, I think I'm in love with him."

He smiled quickly.

"No, I think, I don't know. I think I'm just a job for him." She blew her nose and reached for another tissue.

"Sweetie, if I know anything about that man, it's that he never mixes business with pleasure. He has a reputation, one of being strictly business. Why do you think I hired him in the first place?"

He used his finger to pull her chin up until she looked at him in the face. "If he mixed pleasure with business, then I can guarantee it had nothing to do with the job. He took you to see his family in Washington, right?"

She nodded her head and wiped away a tear with the back of her hand.

"A man doesn't fly you halfway across the continent to visit his family without there being something there. Trust me."

She smiled at her dad. Maybe he was right.

"Besides, he's still on the job. At least until I tell him he's done. That was part of the deal."

She smiled again. "Thanks, Daddy. I knew you'd have all the answers. What can I do now?"

"Well, if he doesn't come back on his own… If I know anything about my little girl, you'll find a way to make him crawl back."

That night she lay in her bed for a few hours listening to the sounds of the city around her. She missed the sounds of the jungle and of David sleeping beside her. She missed his warmth, his smell, his touch.

She knew she was going to have a hard time falling back into a pattern. How could she ever go back to a normal life after what they'd been through? Did she want to?

More importantly, did she want to do it all alone? Even though they'd only known each other a few months, she couldn't stop thinking about him.

The shadows on her ceiling did little to soothe her as the light hit the leaves that were starting to fall from the large tree outside her window. She turned and hit her pillow a few times, trying to get comfortable. She'd had no problem sleeping in the dirt or wet sand last week. Why was her pillow-top mattress that she'd spent a fortune on so uncomfortable now.

Damn him for making her feel like she wasn't good enough. Damn him for walking out. Her father was right, maybe she needed to make him crawl back to her. She knew he was probably out there, sitting somewhere watching her place.

After all, he was still working on security details for her dad.

She'd just have to come up with a plan that would get him back into her life.

She knew what she wanted now, and if it meant playing dirty, she'd just have to get dirty again.

David sat in the rented van, checking all his monitors. There were only a few lit up right now, since he hadn't had the time to put any cameras in Alice's condo yet.

Okay, he had to admit it, he'd had some time after her family left, he just didn't have the guts to walk up there and knock on her door.

The cameras he did install he'd waited a few hours after all her lights had gone out to put up.

He had a nice view of her front door and all the windows to her place. He'd tried to angle them so he'd be able to see inside, but she'd shut all her blinds.

Good girl. Her safety was supposed to be his goal, but he wished he could be there, lying next to her. Maybe he'd misjudged her reactions? She'd been quiet on the trip home.

Maybe she was just thinking about her work and not their relationship?

Then he remembered how she'd reacted when her father had called. No, she was either embarrassed that they were together, or… he didn't know. He was trying to fool himself that her reactions were anything but what he'd witnessed.

She didn't want to be with him anymore and it was as plain as the nose on his face.

He'd been a fool not to tell her how he felt about her before they'd left Washington. Thinking about it, maybe it was a good thing he hadn't told her.

Maybe she would have just laughed at him? No, he'd learned a lot of things about Alice over the last few months and she wasn't a vicious kind of person.

He could imagine her explaining how he wasn't really in love with her.

Maybe she'd even interrogate him as to why he thought he was in love with her?

He chuckled at the idea of her holding him under a bright, hot lamp trying to get the truth out of him.

He remembered how she'd been with his parents and smiled. No, she wasn't just blowing him off. Maybe she just needed some more time to think about her feelings?

After all, they'd only known each other for a short period of time. He knew he was jumping into things quickly. But he didn't need a lot of time to decide she was what he wanted. After all, he'd never felt remotely this close to another woman before.

He had to think of ways to get her to see what she wanted. That he was what she wanted. There had to be some way he could make her see what he'd already discovered. He knew he'd been too chicken to blurt out his feelings. He was a guy after all.

He'd been teased by his buddies when he'd been bit on the butt by a spider and had gotten hospitalized. Imagine them finding out that he wanted to tell Alice that he loved her and wanted to spend his whole life with her. He'd probably never hear the end of it.

He knew that when Tom, one of his buddies, had gotten married a few years back, he'd been tormented by the whole group. They'd all attended his wedding and got drunk and had a blast.

Tom had just smiled and told them that he'd get them back at their weddings. That's what friends did. He leaned back in the seat and tried to prop his feet on the small countertop.

When his cellphone rang, he was surprised to see the international code.

"Ivan?"

"Yeah, man." David laughed. Ivan never really talked in his native tone.

"What are you doing back in Jamaica?"

"Trying to hide from my future wife."

David coughed and sat up. "What? You're getting married?"

"Not if you can help a brother out. Please tell me you need some help. I can do all your dirty work. I'll even run and get you coffee. Just get me the hell away from my parents' meddling ways."

He looked at the empty monitors and jumped at the chance. "Ivan, why don't you hop on the next plane to Texas?"

After hanging up the phone, he sat back and smiled. Ivan was just what he needed. Someone Alice could relate to. Someone she trusted. Someone he trusted.

It helped that Ivan had been through heartbreak a few years back. He was still open to the idea of falling in love.

Maybe he had some insights into what he could do, how he could wear her down. Maybe even how he could tell her how he felt.

As he waited for the sun to rise, he thought about how many ways he could get back with her.

Finally, he had his opportunity. He watched as she crossed the street alone.

He was sitting in the car next to his shooter. He knew the man could easily do this next job, but he didn't want anything to get messed up, so he was sitting in the car with him.

"We may have a problem," his man said as he pointed to a van on the opposite side of the street.

Then he could see it. The large man who'd been the cameramen in Rio was sitting in a black van watching Alice cross the street.

"I told you he was security."

"He can't watch her all the time." He looked down at his watch and noticed he was running late. "I'm late. Follow her, grab her if you can. If not, text me and we'll continue with the backup plan."

They watched Alice drive away in her car, followed closely by the dark van.

Then the man got out of his car and ran to his vehicle.

The next morning Alice marched into her office with a plan. There was no way she was going to let Anthony fire her. She walked out of the elevators and past the secretary with her head held high.

She avoided talking to anyone; she just wanted to make it into her office. She was so focused on getting there, she didn't see the man sitting behind her desk until after she'd closed the door, leaned back on it, and released a sigh of relief.

"Was it that bad?" Steve asked from her chair. She couldn't help it, she squealed. She'd only met Steve Myers once before, on the day she'd been hired almost five years ago.

He was an older gentleman with silver hair. His suits always looked pressed, and he never had a hair out of place. He had a reputation for being a hard-ass and she'd done everything she could to avoid dealing with him directly.

"Oh," she stood up straight and ran her hands over her skirt, trying to make sure, she looked perfect.

"Come in, Miss Rhodes. I'd like to hear all about your adventures."

She walked in and sat in one of the chairs that sat in front of her desk. She felt nervous, like she was being interviewed for a job. This was her office, but she didn't quite know what was going to happen next.

Less than an hour later, the laughter could be heard down the hall from her office. Alice realized a few things talking to Steve.

First, he was a cool guy for a hard ass. Second, he only wanted what was best for his business and his employees.

He'd told her that he had set up a fund for Mark's and Joe's families. Even though the business had nothing officially to do with their deaths, he'd promised to take care of them, something she'd almost broken-down crying over. She'd missed their services since she was still hiking through the jungle trying to save her own skin at the time.

Steve had also told her that he was very interested in running her piece on Hector, especially considering her father's new campaign. It would shed some shed more light on the whole subject of the struggle with the drug lords. Not to mention the effects his new law would have on stopping drugs from coming in through one of the largest states, one that had problems with border patrols.

The fact that Texas has the most drug seizures through traffic stops weighed heavily on her father's campaign. Steve was a huge supporter of her father and had dedicated the network to covering his upcoming speeches.

Alice didn't know if Steve treated her special because of her connections, but she didn't think so. She liked to think that Steve was just a really good guy, who'd been judged by the wrong people.

"You understand that the story idea still needs to be run by the board. I'll let you know when they decide. It should be sometime later this week."

He stood and shook her hand. "Again, I'm sorry about everything that's happened to you over the last few weeks. If you need any more time off, please, just let us know."

She smiled and shook his hand. "Thank you, no. I'm ready to get back to work and keep busy."

She needed to so she could stop thinking about the one person she still couldn't get out of her mind.

Later as she made her way to the supermarket, she was so preoccupied with her thoughts that she didn't realize she was being followed.

At first, she thought she was hallucinating. Then she'd purposely gone into the frozen food section and opened one of the large glass doors. There he was, looking back at her through the reflection.

Hector stood at the end of the aisle, but when she turned to look, he was gone. She'd rushed to the end of the aisle but hadn't seen him or anyone else for that matter.

As she walked out to her car, she was shocked to see Ivan leaning against her car. She'd rushed to him and hugged him. When he told her he was working with David to watch her, she'd been a little upset that David wasn't going to do it himself.

"Don't look like that, Princess." The use of David's nickname shook her.

"Sorry, that's what he calls you." He smiled and she realized she couldn't be mad at him. "He wants me to watch you when you're out."

Plus, I'm supposed to install surveillance in your place. I wanted to wait until you got back."

"Well, I'm just heading back now. Were you following me earlier? In the store?"

He nodded his head. "Did you happen to see a large Latino man, gray hair, a little taller than you?"

He looked at her and thought about it. "No, but then again, I wasn't looking for a Latino man. Should I be?"

She looked around the full parking lot and shook her head. "No, I think my mind has been playing tricks on me. Come on, let's go put up cameras for David."

"That was too close. Now there is a big Jamaican watching her as well. I think she spotted me in the store."

"I don't care. I've just found out that I might have a chance to get my hands on her at the end of this week. I'll keep you posted." He clicked his phone shut and smiled as he thought about literally getting his hands on her.

Damn, he was a fool. It was two nights later, and he was sitting in a dark van across from Ann's condo, watching her on the monitors. Ivan sat next to him, chewing on a handful of peanuts.

"Thanks again, man, for handling my situation. I really needed to get out of there. My parents were trying to get me married off again." His friend shook his head in horror.

"Marriage to you would be a nightmare." Ethan mumbled.

"I'm sorry. What?" His friend crushed a handful of peanuts in his palm.

David laughed for the first time in two days. He thought his friend knew something was up with him. It wasn't as if he couldn't handle the simple job on his own, it was more like he didn't want to anymore. He needed the moral support of a man who'd fallen once. Boy had Ivan fallen.

She'd been the "African Beauty to beat all others," or so his friend had called her. David had been shocked that a woman so beautiful could have ever fallen for his friend.

It was thanks to that woman, Leena, that he'd deserved the two punches from Ivan in Ponce. David couldn't let her get away with the diamond heist.

After all, it was his job to catch the bad guy, even when the bad guy turned out to be wearing four-inch daggers and sleeping with his best friend.

His mind kept playing over so many questions. He was back to questioning Alice's motives at this point. Sometimes he'd think he'd figured it all out, but then he'd be persuaded in the opposite direction.

It was as if he was playing devil's advocate with his emotions.

Was Alice any different than Leena had been? She'd acted grateful to him about rescuing her in Ponce.

She'd spent all that time with him in Guatemala acting like they were closer than he'd ever been with anyone else. Hell, he'd taken her to meet his family!

Maybe it was all in his mind? Maybe he was the reason she had pulled away?

If he had said or done something… He thought back to all the time he'd spent with her.

Maybe she had played him? Maybe she was just getting through her survivor's guilt by sleeping with him.

He closed his eyes as he listened to her talk on the phone. The wiretap and cameras were something he'd made Ivan do.

Then he remembered Alice's face when she'd seen his friend. It had lit up and she'd hugged him like he was an old friend. Maybe it was all just an act?

"You're being too hard on her, you know."

David glared at Ivan from across the small space.

"You should listen to me; I know what I'm talking about."

"Right, because your relationships have worked out great so far." David turned back to the row of monitors. Each screen showed a different scene in Alice's condo.

Ivan punched him lightly on the arm. Even though it was a light punch, David knew he'd have a small bruise there by the morning.

"Do what you will, old friend, but in case you haven't noticed, we are getting much older. You won't be able to do this kind of job much longer. I'm planning on retiring soon."

"Ivan, you've been planning on retiring since I met you eight years ago."

Just then, David watched as a red, Honda Civic pulled up to Alice's curb.

A young kid around the age of twenty jumped out carrying a large red pizza box.

"I'll be back. I'm going to check it out." David slid open the door open quietly and reached the kid before he could ring Alice's doorbell.

Paying the kid too much, he stood and looked down at the pie.

Maybe he was being too hard on her? He stepped back and rang her doorbell.

Waited to see what her next move would be.

Chapter 16

Returning Home

A lice was bored. Since returning home, she'd gone to work, gone to the grocery store. Her kitchen was now fully stocked with groceries. When she'd arrived home last night she had realized there wasn't anything to eat since she'd left for a long journey.

She'd visited her family and done other boring everyday tasks but was still bored out of her mind. How could she ever get back in the swing of a normal life after what she'd gone through with David?

She'd been happily surprised to see Ivan yesterday at the store. When they'd come back to her place; he'd come in and installed several small cameras throughout her place.

She'd talked to him and had found out that he'd had to leave Ponce on account of helping them escape. She felt bad but was happy that he was going to be helping David out now.

She was in the middle of watching the evening news when the doorbell rang.

She hadn't even heard a word the announcer said since she'd been too busy thinking of David again.

Knowing it was the pizza man at the door, she rushed to grab her new purse.

She'd ordered online since she knew her phones were being listened to. She opened the door without looking out the peephole.

Then she was pushed up against the door and pinned there as she stared into David's very angry face.

"You didn't even check to see who it was?" He growled out, pushing her against the door further. He kicked her front door shut with his foot. Then he used his arms and pinned her hands beside her body.

She could see the anger in his face, and she was beginning to feel angry herself. How dare he leave the other night? He hadn't even talked to her, just left her like she'd been some job. The least he could have done was say thanks for the hot sex while we ran for our lives.

Then he'd hired Ivan to deal with her because he was too chicken to deal with her himself.

Using that anger, she pushed her hands away from the door and used her best Judo moves on him. She was free from his grasp in only a few seconds.

Then she was pinned against the wall beside her front door. Damn, he was good. She almost smiled at his moves. She was still angry at how cowardly he'd been.

She tried a second time, this time making sure not to turn her back to him. She ended up pushing him back a full step. He looked at her as if he was impressed.

Then he came at her, and she avoided his hands by twisting, then blocked his legs as he tried to swoop them out from under her. She was so happy that she'd avoided the maneuver, she hadn't seen the next move coming.

She ended up flying and landing on her back on her plush carpet. The wind was knocked from her slightly as she landed. He'd held her hips and had taken most of the blow with his knees, which were on either side of her hips, pinning her down. Her arms were grasped tightly in his hands as he held them up beside her head.

"Is this how safe you are? Opening the door without looking?"

She tried to kick him off her, and using her hips, she bucked until she was running out of breath. She realized she was getting nowhere. Blowing the hair out of her face, she glared up at him.

"Fine, you win. Now let me up."

"No, not yet." He leaned over until his nose was less than an inch from hers.

"Was I just a game to you?"

When she looked up into his eyes, she saw more than anger there, which totally broke her. Her entire body went soft.

"No! Was I just a job to you?" She lifted her chin, challenging him. She held her breath, waiting for his answer.

He pulled back a little and looked deep into her eyes. She couldn't read his thoughts, but she had seen the anger drain from his eyes.

"Ivan, sign off for the night. I've got this." David pulled a small ear bud out of his ear and set it on her coffee table. Then he was kissing her, and she had the wind knocked out of her lungs for the second time in less than five minutes.

"I thought you didn't want this." He pulled her head back, exposing her neck as he ran his mouth down her skin. She pushed on his shoulders until she rolled him over. Then she straddled him, pinning him to the floor, and looked down at him.

"How could I not want this?" She bent down and bit his lip lightly, pulling on it gently. Then she sucked on it, soothing the sting she'd caused.

His hands went to her hips, and he pushed them against him. Using his knees to spread her legs, he pinned her hands over her head and just looked at her.

She needed the speed, she needed him. They rolled across the carpet, removing clothing quickly. She even heard something rip at one point, which caused her to laugh. She moaned as she nibbled her way down his stomach. How she'd missed the taste of him, the feel of his hot skin, vibrating under her hands.

She knew they were going fast, but when he lifted her knees and plunged into her, she stopped caring. She arched her back and screamed with delight as he held her hips and repeated the movement more slowly this time.

Then she looked up into his eyes and saw what she'd tried to deny in herself.

She was in love.

Finally, there was no use denying it any further. Reaching up, she took hold of his face and pulled him down to her mouth. Just before he kissed her, she closed her eyes as a tear escaped.

"Did you want some pizza?" David asked half an hour later. They were lying naked on her floor, their clothes scattered in piles around them. Their breathing had finally calmed down to a somewhat normal level.

"Mmmm, no. Maybe later. Besides, I only ordered it to see what you'd do when it arrived."

He closed his eyes and realized that he'd fallen right into her trap. Then he remembered the monitors. If Ivan was still watching the monitors, he'd have to kill him.

He cringed, remembering that everything that happened in here was neatly being taped. Okay, first on his list, erase the tape, then kill Javan if he watched.

"What's going on in that brain of yours?" Alice asked, looking down at him.

He cringed again.

"How bad would it be if we accidentally just made a porno?"

She laughed. Then she smiled and leaned over him.

"You know, if you hadn't come in to talk to me, I was going to do a nice striptease for one of these cameras, just to get you in here."

He could have sworn she was vibrating. His mind instantly flipped to her slowly removing her clothes for him as he watched in the van. She was starting to rub her hips over him and the friction was going to kill him.

Not wanting any more rug burns on his back, he picked her up and carried her, as she laughed, into the bedroom.

Later, after Alice was asleep, he quietly went out to the van. Ivan had shut everything down, including the tapes before he left. Which meant no porno.

Then he snuck back in the house and back in the bed with Alice and slept until morning, holding her tight against him.

"I can't believe it. It's taken almost a week and they are finally going to let me run my piece from Ponce. They want it edited a little more and some more back story, but the executives want it by Friday."

Alice was so nervous. She began to pace in her small office.

David sat across from her and looked bored. "Are you listening to me?" She picked up the nearest item, which happened to be a stress ball, and tossed it at his head.

He caught it and proceeded to squeeze it playfully as she smiled.

"I'm always listening. I knew they were going to run it. It's a good piece.

Plus, you had an excellent cameraman." He smiled and tossed the ball back at her.

She caught it and set it back on her desk, then walked around and sat in her chair. There was so much to do in the next few days, she didn't think she'd have time.

Preparing a piece this big took a team and her team… she closed her eyes on the flash of memory that popped into her head.

Well, her team was dead.

"I'm going to spend the next few days going over our footage from Ponce.

There must be something else there I can use."

"Do you want any help?" He sat up a little.

"You? Really?"

"Well, I was working here up until my cover was blown. I know my way around the editing room and equipment."

She thought about it and realized he was right. When he'd been undercover, she'd never once questioned his abilities as a photographer or editor. Just as a human being.

Just then her phone rang, and seeing the number on the screen, she smiled.

"Hi, Daddy,"

"Hi, sweetie. Don't forget the dinner tonight at the Kramer's. It's at eight sharp. Oh, and sweetie, bring David."

Her smile got bigger. She had forgotten the dinner. Her father was campaigning again, and she knew that meant lots of wine and dine situations.

She couldn't always make them, but the Kramers were very old family friends.

Plus, it was a white tie sort of dinner, and she was just dying to see what David looked like in a tux.

"We'll be there." When she hung up the phone, she watched David's eyebrows shoot up in question. She tilted her head and imagined what it would be like seeing him dressed in a tux.

"Tell me, Mr. Bond, do you own a tux?"

He smiled quickly. "All of us double O agents have them. Why?"

He stood around her condo waiting for her to come out of the restroom. He didn't mind getting dressed up for occasions and always saw it as a challenge to hobnob with the upper crust. He looked at it all as if it was part of his training, seeing if he could fit in anywhere.

He knew he could fit in the jungles, the deserts of the Middle East, the slums of any large city, and the beaches at the best resorts. How different was wearing a monkey suit with the high rollers in politics from pretending to be a male stripper in Vegas?

He smiled thinking about it. Then his smile fell away as Alice walked out of the restroom.

The dress was the color of her blue eyes. He swore he could see right through it and when he looked at her, he saw her nipples peek through the light material towards him.

He felt his tuxedo pants getting too tight. Damn, they'd been specially made for him and now he felt like he couldn't breathe.

Her hair was piled up in some sort of fancy bun. There were long dark twists falling around her face, making him itch to feel the silky softness of it in his fingers.

His eyes roamed from her head down her long form to her feet, which were exposed in sexy little heels with sparkly stones that showed her newly painted toenails. He wanted to tear everything off her and lick her from head to toe.

"Well?" she said and did a little turn. The back of the dress was worse than the front. It dipped down to the middle of her back, exposing her entire back, showing off her silky skin.

"Well?" He repeated. He didn't know what to say. It was like every cell in his brain had just left him to go on vacation. "You ... You look beautiful."

She smiled quickly and walked over to grab her small silver purse from the table.

"Are you sure we must go to this thing tonight? I'm not feeling too hot.

Maybe we should just stay in?" He walked over to her, pulling her close. When he got closer, he smelled her perfume and closed his eyes on a moan.

Not only did she look good, but she also smelled good. Which got him wondering if she tasted just as good. He started to dip his head to have a taste when she stopped him with her hands.

"Oh, no, you don't. You are not going to mess this all up. It took me two hours to look like this." She held his head at bay.

"Just one lick. Just to see if you taste as good as you look."

She laughed. "You can taste me later. Right now, we're going to be late if we don't leave now."

He pulled back and took her hand and made a point to bow from his waist.

"As you wish, my lady." He brought her hand to his lips and kissed her lightly.

Then he turned her wrist around and kissed the inside of her wrist, pressing his tongue to the inside of her sensitive skin.

He stood back up and smiled. "I knew it. You do taste good."

She laughed at him. "Idiot."

He took her arm, and they walked out of her condo together.

At two minutes past eight precisely, they walked in the Kramer's front door.

The luxurious house was situated in the upper-crust neighborhood of Austin. The mansions were the size of whole city blocks here.

Alice could remember playing in the pool in their back yard as a child during some hot summers days. Their sons, Brian, and Brett were some of her closest friends growing up. The twin boys now were practicing law in Houston.

She enjoyed dressing up for special occasions and tonight she was dressed in her deep blue spaghetti strap number, which hugged her in all the right places.

David was in a tux that looked like it was made just for him, and probably was. It fit him perfectly and he looked very handsome, like he was born wearing it.

She'd yet to do anything with her hair color and in truth, she kind of liked the darker look.

She'd curled it slightly and pushed most of it on top of her head so it could fall in ringlets around her face. The darkness of it accented her skin and eyes or so her stepmother had said when she'd first seen it.

She'd had a huge problem with her father marrying again after her mother's death, but after Blake was born, she stopped giving her dad so much grief over it.

After all, she'd always wanted a brother. Coleen, on the other hand, Alice still couldn't stand. She tried to avoid spending too much time with the woman, who happened to be only a few years older than her.

The fact that Coleen called her sweetie, her father's favorite nickname, just plain annoyed her.

The woman always treated her like she was a child, which was stupid in Alice's mind. Coleen would give Alice advice on her clothing, her hair, and even tried once to give her advice on her career.

At one point, the woman tried to treat her like a sister. Thankfully, Alice set her straight before that went any further.

Over the last few years since Blake's kidnapping, Coleen was starting to act a lot more like a mother figure to Blake than just an older sister. So, Alice had cut her a little slack.

The Kramer's dinner was always an important one for her father's campaign.

She knew most of the people attending and liked only a third of them. The rest were powerful people and to be honest just plain rude. She tried avoiding most of them, but somehow ended up chatting with the worst offenders most of the time.

Tonight, being on David's arm, she felt more powerful. When they walked up and started talking to her father and Coleen, David had shaken hands with her dad and started talking like they were old buddies.

It was nice seeing the two men she loved in her life getting along and enjoying each other's company.

Her father's new assistant, Paul, was always hovering around him. The skinny man gave Alice the creeps. Not that this was the first assistant of her father's that had given her the creeps, just the worst.

His dark hair was always slicked back. He had a crooked nose that was too big for his face. He could have been good looking if it wasn't for his eyes.

She'd always been one to spot the pretends, the men who said one thing and did another. Maybe that's why she was so good at being a journalist. Paul was hiding something and always walked around like he was laughing at some private joke that only he knew.

She didn't quite know what had happened to her father's last assistant, a striking young redhead. No doubt Coleen had something to do with letting her go, since that's how she got the role of wife to begin with. Going from being her father's assistant to being pregnant by him had secured her next role as wife.

Alice was standing near the patio doors waiting for David to bring her a drink when Paul walked up to her.

"I hear you had an exciting time in South America?" He was standing too close for her liking. When she tried to back up, she realized her back was already against the wall. Wishing David would hurry up with her drink, she tried to soothe the man with a slight nod.

He must have taken the gesture as an invitation because his hand reached up and toyed with one of the loose strands of her hair. He was running it through his fingers, and she felt a shiver run down her spine.

"I see you changed your hair color. Too bad, I really enjoyed the blond." It gave her a little pleasure knowing that he didn't like the darker color. "Will you be attending your father's news conference on Friday? I know it's supposed to be a very special occasion."

She did not normally attend her father's conferences. Since it was a conflict of interest, she had never covered the conferences herself.

"No, Paul." He cracked a bigger smile, as if he had a secret joke. "If you'll excuse me, I see my boyfriend." She started to walk past him, and he grabbed her arm.

"Boyfriend? Don't you mean your bodyguard? He wasn't even competent enough to save you from the explosion or do anything to save your two colleagues. I heard they were gunned down like dogs."

A smile crept onto his face, and she felt her skin turn to ice. Blinking a few times, she tried to compose herself. Then she yanked her arm from his grasp and walked around him without saying anything.

She met David halfway across the room. Upon seeing her face, he set the drinks down on a table and took her hand and steered her towards the back door. He didn't stop until they'd walked out onto a small patio area reserved for the hired help.

There was a young woman smoking a cigarette there and when David nodded his head, she left quietly through the door.

"What is it?" David pulled her close. She hadn't realized she was shaking and by this time, her breathing was coming in small gasps. The images of her colleagues flashed through her mind over and over.

"It's nothing. I'm just being emotional. I can't believe I let him work me up like this." She closed her eyes and laid her head against his chest. Listening to his steady breathing helped to level her own out.

She didn't realize that he was swaying her until she looked back up at him.

"What are you doing?"

"Dancing." He smiled down at her. "I figured the best way to take your mind off something bad, was to put it on something good. Besides, I've wanted to dance with you for a while."

He smiled at her and then kissed her forehead. "I'm a good dancer; all of us Bond types must be. You know, to woo all the women." She laughed and forgot about Paul and her dead coworkers.

"Have I told you how beautiful you look tonight?"

She looked up at him and then he was kissing her softly under the moonlight and she forgot everything else, except him.

The little bitch. She hadn't even acknowledged him. Besides, after seeing her across the room with her dark hair, the attraction he felt towards her had dissolved.

Picking up his cell phone, he punched the number. "Is everything set for Friday?" "Yes, what about security?" "Don't worry, I have a plan to take care of them." He smiled and knew his day was coming.

Chapter 17

In the Editing Room

Alice and David spent the next few days locked in the editing room. They had gone over every inch of footage that had been uploaded from Ponce before the incident.

There really wasn't anything other than crowd shots they could use. She'd been enjoying their time together. There was hardly a moment when they weren't together. Ivan had even been moved over to watching Blake instead.

David had been spending all his time with her. He slept in her bed, they ate dinner together, they ate breakfast together. He sat across from her when she worked in her office.

They had been spending a lot of their evenings in the editing room together. She couldn't explain it, she just enjoyed spending her time with him. He was easy to get along with, and she didn't want to be apart from him.

She'd woken the other night to an empty bed and had instantly felt empty herself. Then she'd heard him talking on the phone in the other room. She'd quietly rushed in and smiled when she'd seen him pacing her living room. He'd been talking on the phone butt naked. She'd leaned against the wall and just admired him.

He'd been agitated at whoever he'd been talking to, but when he'd spotted her standing there, he'd smiled and hung up without another word. Then he'd carried her back into the bedroom.

Now, as they were on their third evening working on the footage, they'd finally hit a wall trying to fill a minute-long section. She was ready to pull her hair out. It was just a minute's worth of footage, but it had taken them almost eleven hours to get the segment this far.

Then she looked down and saw the original DVD that David had carried out of Ponce sticking out of her bag.

She'd edited the footage with Mark in the van back in Ponce, but maybe there was something else on the DVD they could use to fill some of the time they needed.

David had gone to get them some food from the vending machines. She knew it was probably going to be their dinner, since she doubted, they'd get out of that room for another two hours. She dropped the DVD in the player and started running through everything on it.

She wouldn't have spotted him if she hadn't been thinking about the other night. Feeling trapped in this room reminded her of being trapped against the wall by Paul. She was rewinding a segment of footage of their first night in Ponce when she spotted his face. She hit the pause button and froze, staring at his skinny, smiling face.

What had he been doing in Ponce? More importantly, why was he talking to Hector? No, why was he yelling at Hector? She played the tape forward until the camera slammed left.

Then she rewound it and played it again. Her mind flashed to the day in the grocery store. Maybe it had been Hector? If he wasn't an informant, what was he? Maybe he was the one behind all this?

Maybe he was still working for whichever drug lord was pulling the strings?

"What's this?" David asked from behind her. She was caught off guard and almost jumped out of her seat.

"It's the extra footage from Ponce. Look here." She pointed to Paul. "What's he doing there talking to Hector?"

David sat the bag of potato chips in front of her, along with an unsweetened bottle of tea.

"Here, let me see." He leaned in and took control of the dials.

"We're taking care of things in Austin. The night of his big speech it will all end. Just do your part and trap his daughter away with the story…" David said, reading Paul's lips.

"Damn, then the camera stop. David sat back and stared at the image of Paul and Hector together.

"David, I thought I saw Hector in my grocery store the other day. I thought I'd been followed, but when I got outside Ivan was there and well…. I forgot all about it until just now."

"Alice, where is your dad right now?"

Her mind flashed to an image of her father. Then to her brother's face.

"Alice?" David turned and took her shoulders in his hands. "Come on, Princess. Where is your father?"

She looked down at her watch. Seven forty-five. Friday night. "He's making a speech about his new drug laws that he's going to pass when he is reelected."

"Where?"

"The stadium at the University of Texas. His speech is supposed to start at eight."

"Call him." He put her cell phone in her hand, and she dialed her father's number with shaking hands.

When it went to his voice mail, she shut her phone and tried again. On the third try, she stopped and thought. Then she tried Coleen's cell number. It went to her voice mail, too.

"David, no one is answering."

"Come on." He started pulling her towards the doors. It was a ten minute drive from the studio to the stadium, but with all the people, she knew you could easily tag an extra fifteen on to that time. There was no way they would make it to her father in time.

David used her phone as they ran towards his car.

"Ivan, they're going after the senator. Who's watching him tonight? Damn, okay, call him.

Tell him Paul Green is in on it. Yeah, I know. Okay."

David jumped behind the wheel and peeled out of the parking spot with Alice sitting beside him, her mind whirling through images of them not getting to her father in time.

What did Paul have planned? Why had he waited until now? Then her mind flashed to what he had said the other night at the party.

The phone rang and David answered. "Yeah? When? Damn, how soon can you get there? Yeah, us too. Okay." He set the phone back down.

"Your father's security team isn't answering our calls." David paused as he turn sharply to avoid cars on the highway. She looked down and noticed they were doing eighty and he showed no signs of slowing as he weaved in and out of traffic, avoiding cars and taking turns at ludicrous speeds.

She held onto her seat and knew that he'd get them there on time. He had to get them there on time.

"There, David." She said as they pulled into the university's parking area a few minutes later. She looked down at her watch and noticed it was three minutes before her father would take the stage.

Was there a shooter? Was there a bomb? She didn't know what Paul had planned, but she knew she had to try to get to her father.

When David parked the car, they ran from it, heading straight for the doors to the stadium. There were still people filing in the doors and they had to push their way in. At one point, she lost sight of David, but continued to push through the crowd.

Finally, when she broke through the crowd, she headed towards the field. In the center was a large white stage which had been set up for her father's speech.

Camera crews and TV reporters surrounded the stage, and she watched in horror as her father stepped out onto the stage just as she jumped the fence and hit the grass.

It all seemed to be going in slow motion, and she felt like her feet wouldn't carry her fast enough. She pumped her arms as she ran across the large space. She still felt like she wasn't eating up enough ground.

Where was David? She ran towards the stage at top speed and knew she had to make it. The crowd was loud, but when a man stepped to the microphone and announced her father, everyone cheered, making so much noise it was almost too much to bear. She screamed her father's name over and over, and by the time she reached the stairs at the edge of the stage her father had stepped into the spotlight.

He waved to everyone as they cheered and the second, he began speaking, a light exploded above his head and then all hell broke loose on the stage. She was tossed to the ground by someone, then dragged in a direction away from her father.

She could only see that he'd been hit by the shattering glass, and as blood dripped from his face, he looked over at her and screamed her name.

His plan was working flawlessly. He'd sent the security detail on a wild goose chase. They were so busy down by the stage, they didn't have time to check the upper private rooms, where he and Hector had set up. He stood there and watched Hector set up his scope on the rifle. He normally didn't personally get involved, but he couldn't wait to see this one through.

They were just seconds away when he saw the cameramen, David, running towards the booth. Stepping back into the darkness of the booth, he slipped out his weapon of choice.

The long knife handle was something he'd treasured, as was the blade. He'd always carried it on him, just in case.

Now he stood in the shadows and waited for his revenge on the man who had screwed up his plans from the first day.

David was fighting for his life. There were two of them, he'd spotted them instantly when he'd entered the large stadium. His eyes had scanned not the stage, where Alice was focused, but instead the roof and upper bleachers of the large stadium.

It had taken him only a few seconds to see the dark spot flying in a private booth area. The nose of the rifle stuck out from the box. With his mind totally focused on getting there quickly, he lost track of Alice.

He knew she'd make it to her father and hoped to God she had enough sense to stay down.

When he reached the opening to the booth, he threw himself in and charged the man, covered in darkness. He didn't see the second man come out of the shadows until the knife was already on a downward arch.

Trying to block it, he felt the blade hit his rib cage, tearing his shirt and the skin below. Turning, he connected a solid blow to the skinny man's nose, shattering it and sending blood splattering all over both.

Paul, the senator's assistant, crumbled to the ground in a heap of unconscious man. Then a shot rang out behind him, and he turned his attention back to the sniper.

When the man tried to shoot the rifle again, David's fist connected with the side of his face just as the gun exploded.

David could hear the screams of people, and knew the whole stadium was in chaos, but didn't stop to see if anyone on the stage was hurt. He braced himself for the fight that was sure to come.

"You've ruined our plans. You've been a thorn in our sides since the beginning when I tried to snatch Miss Rhodes in Ponce."

David thought back to the first night he'd followed Alice out of the hotel. It was the night Hector had approached her outside. Hector must have been trying to lure her away with a false story.

"Why take her?"

"With her we would have control over the Senator. We know he would do anything to get his daughter back, including dropping out of the race."

"Why are you so stubborn about the senator dropping out?" He circled the man, waiting for a moment to spring.

"His running mate has better plans that will benefit my employer much more."

"Who is your employer?"

Hector laughed. "You think I would be stupid enough to tell you?"

Hector rushed towards him.

David's fist arched down trying to connect with the man's face, but this time Hector blocked it and threw himself towards David.

The man's punches were as brutal as his own, catching Ethan off guard. He had to concentrate to keep each blow from connecting with his face or ribs, where he could feel blood oozing down his side.

He connected a few good blows, sending Hector falling over a row of seats.

When he came up, David noticed the gun in his hand just before he felt the bullet connect.

David threw himself at the man, not waiting. He hit him with all his strength until, finally, he had the man pinned and was straddling him. Blood was dripping down Hector's unconscious face as David leaned over him.

David's vision blurred just as two uniform cops came running into the room, their guns drawn and pointing right at him. David raised his hands as far as he could, until the pain was too much. He told them he was security right before he passed out.

The security guards that had grabbed Alice dragged her halfway across the field as she screamed and kicked at them. She tried to tell them she was the senator's daughter, but they just didn't listen.

Finally, they let her go after her father rushed forward and yelled at them.

She looked desperately around for David. She asked all the security team and no one seemed to know where he was.

Her father's face needed a few stitches, so they rode together to the hospital.

Alice was so concerned about David she didn't even care that Coleen sat in the back of the car and cried the entire time.

She'd complained about being so close to dying that Alice had rolled her eyes. Coleen hadn't even been up on the stage. She listened as her father comforted her the entire trip to the hospital.

They took her father to a private ER room, and Coleen followed along. Alice was sitting in the waiting area alone when she heard a loud voice and followed it to another room in the ER. She was shocked to see David lying on a stretcher, screaming and fighting off a nurse and doctor.

Rushing to his side, she noticed all the blood and felt herself turning pale.

"Oh my God, David! Are you okay?"

She tried to push the nurse who was trying to hold David down out of the way. When he saw her, he went still.

"Are you, okay?" he asked at the same time. She nodded her head and then noticed the hole in his chest as the doctor tried to hold his hands over the open wound. Then she noticed blood dripping from a large gash in his side.

"David! You've been shot!" He smiled a little at her obvious assessment.

"I've had worse. I just needed to know that you were all right. What are you doing here?" he asked.

She could see his color slowly starting to drain. His eyes looked cloudy and she could tell he was slowly losing focus. "My father needed stitches. He was hit by some breaking glass. He's all right. Everyone else is all right."

The nurse moved aside so she could hold his hand. Ann watched as she moved to his other side and started helping the doctor who was trying to stop the bleeding.

"We need to get Mr. Smith into surgery. Are you his…?"

"Wife, she's, my wife. I want her in recovery, I want her there when I wake up," David growled before she watched his eyes slide closed.

"Sorry, Mrs. Smith, we've given him something to knock him out. He was putting up quite a fight," the young nurse apologized.

"How ... How bad is it?" she asked the doctor as they started to wheel him down the aisle.

"We'll know more once we get inside. Please, wait just there. I'll come find you once we know more." He pointed towards a private waiting area.

Over the next three hours, Alice sat in the waiting room with her father and Coleen. Blake showed up shortly after with Ivan and everyone sat waiting.

Coleen had gone and gotten them some takeout dinner and coffee. For the most part, everyone sat in silence. Even Blake sat still. Well, as still as a teenage boy could.

Of course, it helped that he had his PSP to play, but she could tell he was as worried as everyone else. This was his hero that was hurt, the man that had saved him five years ago. The man that had saved her just a few weeks ago.

The man who had just saved her father tonight.

In the evening, the police came in to interview her. She explained how they had found out about the assassination attempt, and why David was there in the room with the two men, Paul, and Hector.

She told them she didn't know anything more than that. She'd arranged with her boss, Anthony, to have a copy of the tapes taken to the station for evidence.

"I can tell you both men are currently in the hospital. Just down the hallway. Don't worry, they are under guard. Your husband did quite a number on them."

She smiled slightly, thinking about the possibility of being David's wife. It felt good to have people talk to her as if she was already married to him. She didn't know what she'd do if he died.

After the police left, she sat down, and tears silently slid down her face. Her father walked over and wrapped his arm around her. His forehead was bandaged, and it appeared he'd have a black eye in the morning.

She couldn't stop worrying. She didn't know how extensive David's wound were, but she did know that any bullet to the chest could be a death sentence.

She took the time and called his parents on her cell phone to update them on what was going on. They told her they would fly down on the next available flight and would call Roberta and Ric and let them know.

She was pacing the floor almost three hours later, when the doctor came back in. "Mrs. Smith?"

Everyone in the room looked at her as she rushed over to the man. "How is he?"

"He's stable. We have him in the ICU. You'll be able to see him in a few minutes.

The nurse will come in and take you back to him. He was lucky. The bullet shattered a few ribs and bounced off, leaving a trail we had to follow, but it finally rested in the back of a rib, and we were able to remove it and stop all the bleeding.

The knife wound shattered another rib on his other side. He'll be sore and he'll need to stay off his feet for a few months, but he'll recover."

She closed her eyes and released a sigh of relief.

Chapter 18

The Pampering

David watched Alice fluff his pillows for what seemed like the hundredth time. He smiled, enjoying her pampering him. He knew she was just concerned about him and he enjoyed every minute of it. It had been a close one. So close he'd planned, one he had yet to talk to her about. There had hardly been a time when they were alone.

When he'd woken in the ICU, she was there and so were a half dozen nurses.

Then when he'd come to again, he'd been in a private room with his parents hovering over him. It had been nice having them there, but he wished for some time alone with Alice.

Then she had left for the evening, promising she'd be back first thing in the morning. She had walked in five minutes after his parents and Roberta had.

Now her family was there, chatting and acting like he was a hero.

Blake was there as well. The kid had grown tall, but still looked the same.

David could tell he was glad he was okay, even if he played it cool. Ivan had even stopped by at one point before heading out to his next job somewhere exotic.

David had had enough of running and being shot at in his life. He knew he had a good team of men that would easily take the field for all the upcoming jobs. He could afford to sit back and play boss for a while. It's what he'd always known would happen one day.

That's why he'd been smart enough to hire his close buddies to work with him. Every one of them he could trust, completely.

He knew what he wanted now, and she was sitting in the corner smiling at him. He only needed a minute to be alone with her. So far, it just hasn't happened.

Alice's father had a clue. He is what was happening. That Hector and Paul will pay.

They had both been released from the hospital into police custody. Apparently Paul had been the brains behind the whole deal. The plan had been to kidnap Alice in Ponce and hold her until her father resigned from the race.

Alice was doing an interview that evening with her father, where more details of the whole ordeal would be revealed.

David had known when he'd seen Paul in the private booth that he'd been the one pulling the strings.

The man had bothered Alice the night of the party, and he wished he would have checked him out more then.

Apparently, his whole background check had been pieced together. Hector on the other hand had targeted Alice that first night, trying to get her by herself. Then when she'd shown up the next day with the team, he'd tried to just back out.

David remembered the man being agitated about seeing the three men with her. He should have known then that something was up.

Honestly, when he thought about it, the whole thing had been his fault. If he'd just been better at his job; he would have seen through the man during his interview.

He'd accounted for the man's nerves as fear of being found out. Spending a lot of his time in the hospital bed, his mind wandered over the whole adventure. If he had a chance to go back and change anything, he knew he wouldn't.

He replayed images of Alice standing under the waterfall, smiling. Of her leaning against a tree with a shocked look as he sliced the snake in half. Her smiling as she lay in the sun in Guatemala. Also, of her laughing with his parents on the beach.

He looked over at her now as she talked to her father across the small hospital room. No, he wouldn't change a thing.

Alice had a lot to deal with over the last few days. With David in the hospital she had taken time off from work. Even after everything that had happened, Steve had wanted to run her story.

Of course, they had edited the tapes and used footage of the shooting along with an exclusive interview from her father. She had done the interview personally.

Usually, she didn't mix her personal life with interviews, but Steve and Anthony had asked her, and her father had wanted her to do it. Especially since it was such an important interview.

Her father's running mate had dropped out considering some new information brought to their attention by her father's old assistant, Paul.

Hector had yet to talk, but Paul was chatting away. He wanted an exclusive interview with Alice. Alice, where he promised to tell all. She turned it down.

After the interview aired, she told Steve and Anthony that she was taking a month off. They'd both smiled at her and agreed that she deserved it.

She enjoyed seeing David's family again and since they were there, she had enlisted them to help her out. His mother almost jumped for joy when Alice explained her plans. Roberta had laughed and eagerly joined in the coup.

Next, she had some planning to do. She'd found out some other important information and had set up a schedule. Now all she needed to do was kidnap an ex-Special Forces agent.

Over the next few days, David still couldn't find the right moment to talk to her. There were plenty of times they were alone, but it just didn't feel right.

Every time he'd open his mouth to say something, she'd look at him certain way and he'd shut his mouth again. He'd end up saying something completely different.

The nurses had wrapped his ribs tightly and frequently checked his incision where they'd removed the bullet.

He was tired of being poked and checked. All he wanted to do was go home with Alice, to start their new lives together.

His family stayed for two days, and he enjoyed seeing everyone again, though being stuck in a hospital room wasn't really his idea of enjoying a visit from them.

After they left to go back home, the place almost felt empty. Finally, a day later, he was released from the hospital. He was so excited to get away from all the needles and nurses, he hadn't quite thought about what was next.

A nurse had wheeled him out of the hospital and right into Alice's car, so he found himself sitting in her car on the way to her condo.

Since he was still very weak from all the pain medications, they had him on, he rested his head and thought about his plans.

Maybe he'd ask her over dinner? Maybe when they were lying in bed? He thought of a million words he wanted to say to her, a million different ways to ask her to take a chance on him.

Could someone like her ever be happy with someone like him? Sure, he'd had his share of adventure, but now he was looking forward to a future minus all the running and guns. Would she still find him worth it?

He could just imagine them sitting in front of the fireplace in Washington.

Snuggling up on the couch watching movies, or her cooking in the kitchen while he sat and watched.

Maybe having a family barbeque. Then, maybe in a year, they'll have children. Images flashed through his mind of kids running in the fields. He also had images of him teaching a son or a daughter how to fish.

They would have her blue eyes and her smile. He smiled thinking about it.

Maybe their kids and Rose would be close. Cousins. He smiled again. Yeah, he could get used to the idea of kids with Alice. He knew he still had a few loose ends to tie up, but he'd tried to take care of most of them over the phone before he'd left the hospital.

Running his own security business from home was going to be a lot different than what he'd been doing over the last few years. He was lucky the only jobs that he'd lined up had already been assigned out to one of his teams.

He'd given Ivan the lead so he could sit back and enjoy some of his time alone with Alice. His business wasn't hurting for jobs. He'd had to turn several down. Now his five-man crew was booked solid for the next year.

Just because he was sitting on the sidelines didn't mean he couldn't control everything. He was looking forward to being a real boss and not just the lead in a job.

He knew it was going to be a big change for him, but he was up for the challenge. He just wondered if Ann was up for having him around full time.

Since he'd met her a few months ago, he hadn't really let her out of his sight.

Now, he realized he'd enjoyed having her there. She'd changed so many things in him that he realized he was no longer the same person he'd been three months ago.

Oh, he still felt the need for adventure. The adventure he was seeking wasn't the bullets and bad guy kind. The adventure he wanted was waking up next to Alice and seeing how many ways he could make her smile.

How often he could make her laugh? He knew he'd always wanted to travel, but he also knew that he wanted to be home. He thought of home as being wherever she was.

Maybe she'd want to stay in Austin. Maybe they'd call Washington home. The place didn't really matter to him anymore. What mattered was that he'd be able to be with her.

When he felt the car slowing, he opened his eyes and was shocked to see where they were. The private jet sat ready for takeoff. He looked over to Alice, who was smiling back at him.

"What are we doing here?"

"Well, the doctor said three weeks of rest, so I booked us a flight somewhere where I know you'll get all the rest you need."

She got out of the car and walked around to help him out. It wasn't that he couldn't get out himself, it was just that she liked to help, so he let her.

"Where would that be?"

"Oh, no! You'll just have to wait and see." She walked around and pulled out two large bags and handed them to the luggage handler, who quickly whisked them away to the waiting jet.

He did a double take and realized it was his private jet sitting there, the one they'd used on the way back from Guatemala.

So, some of his secrets must have gotten out of the bag. She turned and smiled at him.

"Yes, I found out who you had to rescue to get that," she said, pointing over her shoulder at his jet. Then she held out her hand, waiting for him to take it. He took it and pulled her close, ignoring the sharp pain on both of his sides. He hugged her, enjoying the rich smell of her dark hair and the feel of her in his arms.

"Alice?" He leaned back and looked down into her face.

"Oh, no. Not until we get inside." She pulled back further, smiling at him.

Did she know what he was going to ask? How did she know?

He nodded his head and followed her onto the plane.

When they were finally in the air, he looked over at her and decided it was now or never.

"I know what you're going to ask, but I want to say something first," she interrupted.

"Fair enough." A million excuses she might give him for saying no ran through his head.

"David, I've known you for over two months and in that time, we've been shot at, blown up, chased through a jungle, and so much more. I'd like to think that in that time we've become closer than two other normal people would have ever gotten. Our relationship may have started with a lie, but I hope it will never end.

So, whatever it is you have to say, just know that you will always have my heart."

He pulled her closer and kissed her nose. "Alice, will you marry me and make me the happiest man alive?"

She smiled. "Yes, of course I will." She reached up and kissed him deeply.

"Now, will you tell me where it is that we are going?"

She laughed, "No, just because you are retiring and getting married, doesn't mean you don't still need a little excitement left in your life."

Chapter 19

The Retirement

David sat on the sand and watched his wife run out of the surf, heading for him. Her dark hair was a little shorter in a bob around her face, but he still enjoyed the rich color.

As did he enjoyed her new curves that showed nicely in the bright white bikini she wore.

Her wet, toned body could still excite him, even when she was eight months pregnant. It had been almost a year since his incident, and he was still enjoying his retirement and marriage.

Life with Alice was anything but boring. They'd jetted off to his home in southern France so he could recover. They had stayed almost two months and while they were there, they visited Ric's sister, Katie, and her husband, Jason.

They'd also visited Katie's brother Dante and his wife, Airlea, in Italy. But mostly they just relaxed and enjoyed each other.

Then they had come back home and had the extravagant wedding of her dreams where his family and hers came together in Austin to celebrate.

Of course, the ceremony included a bunch of his old buddies who had been very rowdy. Then they had flown to Guatemala to spend their honeymoon there.

Now, Alice was planning on retiring herself, after the baby was born.

They had plans to move to Washington to live in the house he'd built. He knew they'd still travel since they both enjoyed it so much, but maybe after the baby came, they would settle down even more.

He still had calls for jobs every now and then; he'd even gotten a few repeat customers begging for his personal help.

So far, his team has been doing a great job of dealing with anything that came up. He'd even hired a few other guys to deal with all the jobs that had come up after he'd saved the senator.

Alice had been a huge help in getting his business switched over to actually being a business. Sometimes he thought that she enjoyed helping him out more than being a journalist. She talked about running the business full time afterwards.

"What are you thinking about?" She sat next to him in the sand. It took some doing, and some help from him, but finally she settled next to him.

He smiled and pulled her close. "You. Us."

He ran his hand over his son, inside her belly. He looked forward to his next big adventure, becoming a father...

References

La fundación de Ponce. eladoquintimes. 23 February 2022. Accessed 24 February 2022. Archived.

Ponce Carnival 2023 is Puerto Rico's Carnival: El Carnaval de Ponce or Carnaval Ponceño (Ponce Carnival) is Puerto Rico's big traditional carnival. Ponce is Puerto Rico's big southern city, so it is less Americanized than the capital San Juan. New York Latin Culture Magazine. 27 January 2023. Accessed 5 February 2023.Archive.

PONCE CELEBRARA SU TRADICIONAL CARNAVAL PONCEÑO. Noticias de Ponce. 29 January 2020. Accessed 30 January 2020.

CARNAVAL DE PONCE SE LLEVARÁ A CABO UN SOLO DIA, SERA EL DOMINGO 23 DE FEBRERO. Carlos José Vázquez. 9 February 2020. Accessed 24 February 2020.

Carnaval de Ponce será rodante. Voces del Sur. 1 February 2021. Accessed 1 February 2021.

Carnaval Ponceño estrena modalidad "rodante": La edición #163 del tradicional evento, se realizará de manera rodante, con el fin de impactar las comunidades de la Ciudad Señorial. El Sol de Puerto Rico. 1 February 2021. Accessed 1 February 2021.

Ponce Carnival Goes International In its 150th Anniversary Edition. Let's Go to Ponce. Archived 11 March 2016 at the Wayback Machine Ponce Carnival. Retrieved 12 April 2010.

A Puerto Rican Carnival: How to Dress for the Ponce Carnival; Introduction: What is a Carnival? The Smithsonian Institution. 1993 and 2002. Accessed 1 February 2019.

Attendance Retrieved April 12, 2010.

Carnaval Ponceño y escultura de arena por Travel Channel. El Sur a la Vista. Ponce, Puerto Rico. 5 August 2011. Retrieved 27 August 2011.

Activan plan de seguridad para Carnaval. La Perla del Sur. Ponce, Puerto Rico. 15 February 2012. Retrieved 1 February 2018.

Activan plan de seguridad para Carnaval. La Perla del Sur. Ponce, Puerto Rico. 15 February 2012. Retrieved 21 February 2012.

Carnaval, Carnival, Llego el Carnaval! Archived 2 October 2013 at the Wayback Machine El Señorial. Ponce Municipal Government. "Anuario: Carnaval Ponceño 2013." February–March 2013. Page 18. Retrieved 30 September 2013.

Tradiciones de la Perla del Sur: Fiestas del Carnaval de Ponce. Archived 20 June 2012 at the Wayback Machine Government of the Autonomous Municipality of Ponce. Retrieved 7 July 2012.

Mantienen viva la tradición carnavalesca. Reinaldo Millán La Perla del Sur. Ponce, Puerto Rico. 6 February 2013. Year 31. Issue 1523. Page 24. Retrieved 6 February 2013.

Tradiciones de la Perla del Sur: Fiestas del Carnaval de Ponce. Archived 20 June 2012 at the Wayback Machine Government of the Autonomous Municipality of Ponce. Retrieved 7 July 2012.

Carmelo Rosario Natal. Ponce En Su Historia Moderna: 1945-2002. Published by Secretaría de Cultura y Turismo of the Government of the Autonomous Municipality of Ponce. Ponce, Puerto Rico. 2003. p. 91.

Celebran 160 años del carnaval en Ponce: Pese a los azotes y las vicisitudes por culpa del huracán María, los ponceños festejarán en grande. Josefina Barceló Jiménez. El Nuevo Dia. Guaynabo, Puerto Rico. 4 February 2018. Accessed 15 February 2018.

Antonio R. Gomez and Margarita Diaz. Unmasking the Ponce Carnival. Daily News. New York, New York. Puerto Rican Day parade Special. 8 June 1995.

Activan plan de seguridad para Carnaval. La Perla del Sur. Ponce, Puerto Rico. 15 February 2012. Retrieved 21 February 2012.

Antonio R. Gomez and Margarita Diaz. Unmasking the Ponce Carnival. Daily News. New York, New York. Puerto Rican Day Parade Special Supplement. 8 June 1995.

The Smithsonian Institution. A Puerto Rican Carnival: How to Dress for the Ponce Carnival. Retrieved April 12, 2010.

Carmelo Rosario Natal. Ponce En Su Historia Moderna: 1945-2002. Published by Secretaría de Cultura y Turismo of the Government of the Autonomous Municipality of Ponce. Ponce, Puerto Rico. 2003. p. 91.

Carmelo Rosario Natal. Ponce En Su Historia Moderna: 1945-2002. Published by Secretaría de Cultura y Turismo of the Government of the Autonomous Municipality of Ponce. Ponce, Puerto Rico. 2003. p. 91.

Cierra La Sonora el Carnaval Ponceño. La Perla del Sur. Ponce, Puerto Rico. 6 February 2013. Year 31. Issue 1523. Page 28. Retrieved 7 February 2013.

Carnival Program Retrieved April 12, 2010.

Travel Ponce Retrieved April 12, 2010.

Unless otherwise indicated, this information is taken from Carnaval Ponceños 2012: Dedicado a los "Ponceños y Ponceñistas destacados en los Medios de Comunicación". Page 34. Municipio Autónomo de Ponce. Oficina de Desarrollo Cultural. February 2012.

Carnaval Ponceño 2012: Dedicado a 'Los Ponceños y Ponceñistas destacados en los Medios de Comunicacion' (Municipio Autonomo de Ponce, 2012; CEE-SA-12-3910), page <no page number; not numbered>.

Ponce celebra su tradicional Carnaval.

Cierra La Sonora el Carnaval Ponceño. La Perla del Sur. Ponce, Puerto Rico. 6 February 2013. Year 31. Issue 1523. Page 28. Retrieved 7 February 2013.

Todo listo para la celebración del Carnaval Ponceño 2014. RadioIsla. 25 February 2014. Retrieved 6 March 2014.

Listo Ponce para los 156 años de su carnaval. Darisabel Texidor Guadalupe. Primera Hora. 25 February 2014. Retrieved 27 February 2014.

Carnaval de Ponce, 2019. (Carnaval brochure - "Edicion 161 del Carnaval Ponceño.") Municipio de Ponce. Oficina de Desarrollo Cultural. Ponce, Puerto Rico. "Reinas del Carnaval Ponceño." p. 14.

Carnaval de Ponce, 2019. (carnaval brochure - "Edicion 161 del Carnaval Ponceño.") Municipio de Ponce. Oficina de Desarrollo Cultural. Ponce, Puerto Rico. "Reinas del Carnaval Ponceño." p. 14.

Este viernes inicia la edición 159 del Carnaval Ponceño. Archived 16 February 2018 at the Wayback Machine WIPR TV. San Juan, Puerto Rico. 22 February 2017. Accessed 15 February 2018.

Celebran 160 años del carnaval en Ponce: Pese a los azotes y las vicisitudes por culpa del huracán María, los ponceños festejarán en grande. Josefina Barceló Jiménez. El Nuevo Dia. Guaynabo, Puerto Rico. 4 February 2018. Accessed 15 February 2018.

Carnaval de Ponce, 2019. (Carnaval brochure - "Edicion 161 del Carnaval Ponceño.") Municipio de Ponce. Oficina de Desarrollo Cultural. Ponce, Puerto Rico. "S. M. Adlin Camille Mendez Vargas." p. 16.

Carnaval Ponceño / Ponce Carnival 2020. BW. Discovering Puerto Rico. Accessed 17 December 2021. Archived.

A punto la histórica versión rodante del Carnaval Ponceño: El gran cierre del evento tendrá lugar en La Playa de Ponce, donde se realizarán las clásicas letanías, el Entierro de la Sardina, la Quema de Júa y la develación del Rey Momo. Ponce, Puerto Rico: Periodico La Perla del Sur. (Printed version: Year 38. Issue 1941. 10 to 16 February 2021. p. 12.) Accessed 10 February 2021.

Carnaval de Ponce regresa a los barrios. Esnoticiapr.com Ponce, Puerto Rico: Periódico Es Noticia. 25 February to 10 March 2022. Year 6. Issue 164. Accessed 25 February 2022. p.14.

Carnaval Ponceño 2012: Dedicado a 'Los Ponceños y Ponceñistas destacados en los Medios de Comunicacion' (Municipio Autonomo de Ponce, 2012; CEE-SA-12-3910), page <no page number; not numbered>.

Ponce celebra su tradicional Carnaval.

Cierra La Sonora el Carnaval Ponceño. La Perla del Sur. Ponce, Puerto Rico. 6 February 2013. Year 31. Issue 1523. Page 28. Retrieved 7 February 2013.

Todo listo para la celebración del Carnaval Ponceño 2014. RadioIsla. 25 February 2014. Retrieved 6 March 2014.

Listo Ponce para los 156 años de su carnaval. Darisabel Texidor Guadalupe. Primera Hora. 25 February 2014. Retrieved 27 February 2014.

Carnaval de Ponce, 2019. (Carnaval brochure - "Edicion 161 del Carnaval Ponceño.") Municipio de Ponce. Oficina de Desarrollo Cultural. Ponce, Puerto Rico. "Reinas Infantiles del Carnaval Ponceño." p. 15.

Carnaval de Ponce, 2019. (Carnaval brochure - "Edicion 161 del Carnaval Ponceño.") Municipio de Ponce. Oficina de Desarrollo Cultural. Ponce, Puerto Rico. "Reinas Infantiles del Carnaval Ponceño." p. 15.

Este viernes inicia la edición 159 del Carnaval Ponceño. Archived 16 February 2018 at the Wayback Machine WIPR TV. San Juan, Puerto Rico. 22 February 2017. Accessed 15 February 2018.

Celebran 160 años del carnaval en Ponce: Pese a los azotes y las vicisitudes por culpa del huracán María, los ponceños festejarán en grande. Josefina Barceló Jiménez. El Nuevo Dia. Guaynabo, Puerto Rico. 4 February 2018. Accessed 15 February 2018.

Carnaval de Ponce, 2019. (Carnaval brochure - "Edicion 161 del Carnaval Ponceño.") Municipio de Ponce. Oficina de Desarrollo Cultural. Ponce, Puerto Rico. "S. M. Gloriangely Velez Batista I." p. 18.

Carnaval Ponceño / Ponce Carnival 2020. BW. Discovering Puerto Rico. Accessed 17 December 2021.Archived.

A punto la histórica versión rodante del Carnaval Ponceño: El gran cierre del evento tendrá lugar en La Playa de Ponce, donde se realizarán las clásicas letanías, el Entierro de la Sardina, la Quema de Júa y la develación del Rey Momo. Ponce, Puerto Rico: Periodico La Perla del Sur. (Printed version: Year 38. Issue 1941. 10 to 16 February 2021. p. 12.) Accessed 10 February 2021.

Carnaval de Ponce regresa a los barrios. Esnoticiapr.com Ponce, Puerto Rico: Periódico Es Noticia. 25 February to 10 March 2022. Year 6. Issue 164. Accessed 25 February 2022. p.14.

About the Author

Norma Iris Pagan Morales was born in Ponce, Puerto Rico. Her parents, Juan Jose Pagan Rodriguez, and Digna Morales Figueroa, now deceased, always helped her with her projects as a writer and teaching career.

Norma had three siblings, Adelin Milagros Pagan Morales, Juan Jose Pagan Morales, and Julio Manuel Pagan Morales. Adelin Milagros Pagan Morales died on February 17, 2023 and Julio Manuel Pagan Morales died on September 19, 1998. He was also known for his writing / composer skills.

Norma did all her academic studies in New York City, Puerto Rico, and Canada. She worked in the City of New York Police Department where she oversaw the full investigation of every new civilian and uniform member of the department.

As an Educator, she worked in New York City Bd. of Education, in Puerto Rico Bd. of Education as an English teacher. She also worked for the Puerto Rico Army National as an English Teacher.

She has teaching certifications for English as a Second Language and Teaching English as a Foreign Language. She also has teaching licenses to teach the following:

1. English Literature
2. Spanish Literature
3. Communication Skills in both English and Spanish
4. Office Procedures = These classes consisted of basic filing to writing memorandums and full company or organization reports.
5. Computers - Certified to teach Long Distance Learning

She has published Thirteen books: Proud of My Puerto Rican Bequest, Porque Soy Boricua? Poemas del Alma, Art in Written Form, A Baffling Short Stories Collection, On Job in the Big Apple, Nature's Rage in the Caribbean, Puerto Rican Soldiers Serving with Pride, Poemas de Ternura and Violence in the City

www.ingramcontent.com/pod-product-compliance
Lightning Source LLC
Chambersburg PA
CBHW021634120626
46545CB00002B/540